Chronicles of the First Empire

QUEEN HORTENSE

Chronicles of the First Empire
Personal Recollections of the Napoleonic Era
With Illustrations by Hippolyte Bellangé

Émile Marco St. Hilaire
and
Hippolyte Bellangé

Chronicles of the First Empire
Personal Recollections of the Napoleonic Era
With Illustrations by Hippolyte Bellangé
by Émile Marco St. Hilaire
and
Hippolyte Bellangé

FIRST EDITION

Leonaur is an imprint of Oakpast Ltd
Copyright in this form © 2013 Oakpast Ltd

ISBN: 978-1-78282-190-8 (hardcover)
ISBN: 978-1-78282-191-5 (softcover)

http://www.leonaur.com

Publisher's Notes

The views expressed in this book are not necessarily those of the publisher.

Contents

Preface	9
A Short Biographical Sketch of Queen Hortense	15
A First Love	30
Hébert	36
Napoleon as Architect	53
An Egyptian Romance	61
The Young Vélite	67
After Jena	73
A Halt During the Campaign in 1815	79
At Erfurt	83
New Year's Day in the Palace of Saint Cloud	89
The Tomorrows	97
Incognito Wanderings	109
A Night at Provins	117
Small Gifts Cement Friendships	122
The Ball and the Fire	128
Waterloo	135
The Emperor's Mother	145

Napoléon, empereur.
GARDE IMPÉRIALE.

Dédié
*À Son Altesse Imériale Le
Prince Napoléon, Avec
mes hommages les plus
respectueuses.*
Constance de la Warr.

Bonaparte, premier consul,
A MARENGO.

Preface

It was during a visit to the dear old-world village of Caudebec en Caux that in a bookshop I chanced upon an old edition of the memoirs of Napoleon by his devoted friend, Émile Marco St. Hilaire, published in Paris in 1842. Greatly impressed by the directness and simplicity of the narrative, and by the many intimate glimpses it afforded of Napoleon at various periods of his extraordinary career, and in circumstances too frequently slurred or ignored by the more formal historians, it was with some surprise that I found the work had not hitherto been translated. Despite the vast extent of Napoleonic literature that has grown up since the death of the exiled emperor ninety-five years ago, (as at 1916), a literature that has been greatly added to within the past quarter of a century, but little apology is necessary for adding to it in an English dress a book so vivid and varied as that in which M. St. Hilaire presented his hero.

For a few years it may be said that Napoleon did "bestride the narrow world like a Colossus," and though close upon a century has elapsed since his death, (as at 1916), the fascination of his personality as one of the great figures of history may be said to have increased rather than diminished with the lapse of time. Students of the man and of the events among which he lived are ever seeking to present anew their differing views of the great phenomenon, but in the chapters of M. St. Hilaire's work we get something more vital and more truly intimate than from any mere presentation resulting from documentary research. He wrote, if not as one of those who came directly within the influence of Napoleon's magnetic personality, at least as one who got his stories from the lips of those who had done so: people who had known the "little Corsican" when the crown of the emperor was still undreamed of, when he was the idolised general winning new glories for the French arms, and that personal devotion from the men he led which was to carry him so far.

It is, I think it will be admitted, by their very intimacy that M. St. Hilaire's stories charm and interest us; they take brief episodes in Napoleon's career and illustrate his character by them, or they take insignificant figures from his entourage and by the devotion of those figures also illustrate his character. And those least given to admiration of Napoleon cannot fail to be struck by the way in which he commanded the most unswerving devotion even of those who attended on him in the humblest positions. This is specially shown in the account of Hébert the barber-soldier, who from barber was promoted to valet, from valet to the position of Steward of Rambouillet—and whose devotion Napoleon remembered to the end, bequeathing him a sum of twenty thousand *francs*.

Something of the same illustration of Napoleon's character, as it was reflected in the devotion of those who worked for him, is to be seen in the story of *The Young Vélite*, and in that of young Zaluski, whose fate might well have inspired Browning's poem, *An Incident of the French Camp*.

Other notable incidents recorded by M. St. Hilaire, which show Napoleon's quickness of sympathy and illustrate his possession of that most valuable gift in rulers, a memory quick to recall people and matters relating to them, may be seen in the account of Napoleon's stay under the roof of the *curé* of Herbisse where he was known, or in the small house in Provins where he was merely "an office" to the good lady, and only known by her to have been the emperor some days after his departure. Indeed, no one can deny the deep sympathy in Napoleon's character—a sympathy which especially showed itself in the interest which he showed in, and his tenderness for, not only his army as a whole, but for each individual soldier with whom he came in contact. Of the way in which that interest was rewarded by the devotion of the soldiers there are many instances in these memoirs, for it is no exaggeration to say that those soldiers were ready to sacrifice their lives for the sake of one tender word or sympathetic glance from their beloved emperor.

But it is not only in the field that these memoirs show Napoleon; they afford, as it were, a series of vignettes in which he is the central figure—vignettes of scenes which if they are mostly ignored by those biographers and historians who deal with the whole life of Napoleon, or the period which he dominated, are no less interesting, no less attractive, no less worthy of our study. That M. St. Hilaire was a devoted admirer of the emperor is certain, and he appears to have lost no opportunity of talking with those whom he met who had been in close relations with Napoleon at widely different periods of his astounding career. Thus, for example, we have an account of one of his first loves, from the lips of one of his fellow officers of the Toulon days, an account which shows him as spending hours looking into the beautiful blue eyes and admiring the slender, graceful figure of an Italian girl; an innocent story of seemingly true affection, though the poor commander in the artillery was already too full of ambition to tie himself in marriage, and that temptation might be removed from his way provided the necessary means for the girl and her mother to return to Italy.

A very different love affair is that vignetted as *An Egyptian Romance* where Napoleon successfully laid siege to the bride of one of his own officers and installed her—"almost Queen of Egypt, and the soldiers called her 'Cleopatra'"—as mistress of his *salon*. In this case Napoleon suddenly deserted his charmer, yet, says M. St. Hilaire, we must not judge from such a fact that he was really fickle, but "only that such events in his great and powerful mind were just fleeting occasions in his life."

Other aspects of Napoleon's life and character, brought out in these too-long neglected memoirs, that are worthy of special note are his constant thought for the beautifying of Paris and his frequent preoccupation with the welfare of the people. We are shown him journeying *incognito* with a single trusted companion about the highways and byways of the capital—sometimes with ludicrous results, as when neither he nor his companion had the money to pay for the breakfast they had eaten; or when he had occasion to complain that the shops did not open early enough. The stories here given suggest that he never shut his ears to any tale of sorrow and distress, and readily disbursed large sums in charity, though the expenses of his household were kept under severe control. With his living interest in the people about him, he was also ever conscious of a desire so to beautify Paris and other cities as to hand down to posterity monuments worthy of the glory of his country—and of this we see something in M. St. Hilaire's chapter on Napoleon as architect, where the emperor is quoted as saying:

> Monuments form the history of nations. Their antiquity is a witness of their civilisation long after its people have vanished, and testifying to their descendants the truth of the victories

they might otherwise not believe in.

Even those who are antagonistic to him will, I think, readily admit that the arrival of the young Corsican in France was the beginning of a new era of prosperity for that country, and that it was through the working of his great brain, combined with his extraordinary power of organisation, that France was finally rescued from the desolation of the Revolution and raised to a new pinnacle of power and glory. I think, too, that even those who are antagonistic to the emperor will find matter to interest them in the varied chapters of the work which I have here translated—a work the simplicity and intimacy of which serve to make it one of such abiding attraction that it is strange it should have waited so long for introduction to English readers.

Gendarme d'élite et Sapeur des grenadiers à pied.
GARDE IMPÉRIALE.

Officier et Soldat des Marins, grande tenue.
GARDE IMPÉRIALE.

CHAPTER 1

A Short Biographical Sketch of Queen Hortense

The dead for whom one prays have, laid on their graves, an Everlasting Flower, they hear distant strains from Heaven—Victor Hugo.

There are names and solemn events which appear to be ignored in their contemporary history, and which have to await a distant epoch after their death to be honoured and appreciated. Praise by historians of the highest qualities to which people can attain is difficult during their lives, as, if excessive, it appears exaggerated to the cold and prejudiced reader; if moderate, it is insufficient and lukewarm to the non-prejudiced. If I only studied my conventional feelings, I should be contented to simply write the following epitaph:

Hortense Eugénie de Beauharnais
Born 10th April, 1 783,
Queen of Holland, 24th May, 1806,
Died Duchess of Saint-Leu,
5th October, 1837,

But such a woman is worthy of more than this. I will leave the task of depicting the historic events in her history to more able and more worthy historians, and will confine myself to mere personal narratives of so noble a life, feeling that absolute facts and accurate accounts are its best praise.

The birth of Hortense took place in Paris in a house occupied by Madame Renardue, Josephine's aunt. Josephine Tascher de la Pagerie had married the Vicomte Alexander de Beauharnais in 1782. In 1787 a rupture took place between Madame de Beauharnais and her husband, so Josephine, whom her grandmother greatly wanted to see again, left for Martinique with her small daughter. They remained there till 1790, when a revolution broke out among the coloured races, with the object of regaining their freedom, and one night the cries of "Fire! Fire!" spread terror in Josephine's home, and in a paroxysm of fear she rose and dragged her child from her bed, rolled a curtain round her, and running out of the house scarcely clothed, made her way through back streets to the harbour, where a French captain gave her shelter in his ship. It was some time before she landed in France, when she proceeded to Paris, and took rooms in the Hôtel des Asturias in the Rue d'Anjou. It was here that the quarrel between Josephine and her husband was made up, as he found how little justification there had been for his complaints against his wife, who explained all to him with dignity and frankness.

Little Hortense never enjoyed happier moments than those which followed this reunion, but, alas, they were short-lived. Her father soon ended his days on the scaffold, and Josephine was dragged to prison. Hortense, left alone with her brother, was in a state of destitution, for her father's possessions had been sequestered and legally sealed, and there was no ready money. Neighbours were kind, and within a few days Madame Holstein, an old county neighbour of Madame de Beauharnais, hearing of their sad position, fetched them from the hotel, and taking them to her apartments tenderly looked after them in every way during Josephine's imprisonment. These first trials in Hortense's life paved the way for her to be able to face bravely those which awaited her in the future.

As soon as Josephine had regained her liberty, she placed her daughter in the famous Pensionnat de Saint-Germain, then under the direction of Madame Campan, whilst her son Eugene's education was entrusted to a tutor. Monsieur Verdière, who lived in Paris. Some months afterwards Madame Campan was commissioned to inform the two children that their mother was about to become Madame Bonaparte, and they were deeply afflicted at the idea of having a step-father, as they both dearly loved Josephine. Hortense remained on at St. Germain until after her mother's return from Italy in 1796, where she had accompanied her husband, who had just been promoted to being "General-in-Chief." She had the happiness also of having Eugene with her, as, although only fourteen, Bonaparte made him one of his *aides-de-camp*. Hortense's life was a very happy one under Madame Campan's care, and her loving and unselfish character endeared her to all her companions. She found friends for life in Mademoiselle Cochelet, who afterwards was her companion and reader, and in Adèle, sister of Marshal Ney, who married Monsieur de Broc, and became Lady-in-Waiting to Hortense when Queen of Holland.

On the return of Josephine from Italy, Hortense left school and lived at the Tuileries with her mother and Bonaparte in a small apartment, most simply furnished. As time went by and Napoleon became First Consul, this simplicity vanished, and the luxury of an embryo Court began to show itself, but Hortense was never elated by it, and led the simple life she arranged for herself. She found great comfort in the perpetual correspondence she carried on with her beloved Madame Campan; to her she confided all her worries and difficulties, which were many in regard to her relations with her stepfather, whose magnetic power and great intellect she could not but admire, but who never gained her affection, although his kindness and consideration for her never failed. The following extracts from one of Madame Campan's letters show a little in what light Hortense regarded him.

> I like to recall, my angel, the wise alarms which the sudden rise in your fortune caused you. They, alas, have been too well justified. Do you remember writing to me: 'My stepfather is a comet, of which we are the tail only, and must follow where it leads. Is it for our happiness? Is it for our misery?' I also remember when your mother found you immersed in your painting at the dinner hour, which the consul insisted on being punctual to the minute, and she impatiently upbraided you, asking if you were training yourself so as to earn your living, you made a true and philosophical reply: 'Why not, dear mother? in the age we are living, who can say what may not be my fate?' My beloved pupil, you know well how deeply my heart is with you in all your difficulties and anxieties, and I only pray that the future may have more happiness in store for you than you anticipate. Your sorrows and joys will ever be shared by me, your ever loving friend.
>
> L. Campan.

Hortense, who daily grew more beautiful, had some of the richest and most illustrious men in France at her feet, imploring to marry her, but none of them touched her heart, and all were refused; but ere long. Napoleon took her fate into his own hands and was determined on her marrying his brother Louis, whom he had brought up and looked on as a son, he being much younger than himself. In this wished-for union politics were far more considered than the feelings of the young people—these his iron will soon overcame, and on January 9th, 1802, the marriage took place in the Chapel of the Tuileries at 10 a. m. in the presence of himself, Josephine, and the Consuls Lebrun and Cambacères. Louis was barely twenty-four years of age, and Mademoiselle de Beauharnais was just nineteen. This union, though to all appearance quite suitable, was later on a source of many trials to Hortense, and her only consolation was in trying to help others in every way she could. The following is an instance of this.

The Marquis de Rivière and Monsieur Lajolais had been parties in the conspiracy against George Cadoudal, and were both condemned to death, but through the prayers and entreaties of Princess Louis, Napoleon forgave them. Napoleon's joy was great when first one son, and soon after a second were born to Hortense, and both were baptized with great pomp at Fontainebleau by Pope Leo VII. A third was born later on. The succession to the empire seemed secure, and they had a magnificent future before them.

Amid all her rapid rise of fortune, Hortense's sweet character remained the same. The Imperial pomp by which Napoleon allowed himself to be dazzled, although his glory required it so little, found her always natural, simple, and indifferent to the exterior grandeur which was imposed upon her. In 1806 fate called Madame Louis to the throne of Holland, and she did not conceal the deep unhappiness it caused her, necessitating as it did her leaving her beloved mother in France. Her departure was marked by an act of charity. Monsieur de Montmorency came to beg her to plead with the emperor for the return to France of Madame de Gévres, whom Fouché had exiled in Switzerland. The queen went to St. Cloud and represented to the emperor the excessive severity of his minister in banishing a woman of over eighty years of age who had no fortune and was a descendant of Duguesclin.

Napoleon listened in silence, and after a few minutes' thought said: "Write immediately to Monsieur de Montmorency that not only do I give Madame de Gévres permission to return to her native land, but as the sole descendant of Duguesclin I will allow her from my privy purse 6,000 *francs* as a pension forestalled by one year. I myself will inform the police." This is a striking homage rendered by the emperor to patriotic valour, which he always loved to recognise.

In Holland in the month of May, 1807, the first great grief befell the queen. Her eldest son died. This grief was deeply shared by Josephine; no one had ever seen her so sorrow-stricken. This was not surprising, as it would be impossible to describe the charming disposition of the boy; also the death of one of the heirs to the Empire seemed in Josephine's eyes to foreshadow trouble for her, as she knew well how eager Napoleon was to feel the succession secured. Often had Napoleon prognosticated the future of France in looking at, or in playing with the children. The eldest of the two was his favourite, as he mostly resembled himself in character.

One day, at the Tuileries, when he had returned from a review, he placed his hat and sword on a chair in his study. The little prince, who was much spoilt by his uncle, took up his sword and twisted its scarf round his neck, and then, putting on the famous three-cornered hat (which covered his face right down to his chin), marched towards the emperor with great importance, and tried to imitate the big drum by loudly shouting, "R-r-ran plan plan!" Napoleon was greatly pleased with little Eugène and tenderly embraced him.

Queen Hortense left Holland to seek, not consolation (for where is the mother who can be consoled for the death of a beloved child), but mitigation of the grief which so overcame her. She settled at Cauderet, a small watering-place, where she soon, as usual, made herself beloved by everyone. She bought off many conscripts, and looked after and gave dowries to poor orphans. In her presence calumny found no place, she knew better than any one how hatred, malice, and envy can poison anyone's reputation, and she never allowed anyone to be badly spoken of. It happened one day that a Dutch lady-in-waiting began abusing some ladies whom the queen received, and called them Orangists and Revolutionists. The queen looked steadily at her, and in a cold voice said:

"*Madame, I* am a stranger here, and am of no party. I receive every one with equal friendship, because I like to think well of everybody. I only have unfavourable impressions of those who speak ill of others."

A fresh sorrow was then soon to envelop the queen. Josephine's divorce was approaching and her courage about to face its greatest trial, and feeling that she required the comfort of her daughter's presence to enable her to endure so terrible a blow, she summoned her to Malmaison. Here she remained until 1813, and it was during her stay that Hortense decided on completely separating from her husband, Louis. Her life with him had been a sad delusion, and he also saw how unsuited they were to each other, so offered no resistance.

Hortense then devoted herself more and more to her beloved

mother, and helped her in all the painful deliberations connected with the divorce. Josephine behaved with calm and proud dignity; no word of prayer for a delay in the sentence passed her lips, not one word of entreaty to retain the Crown fell from them. Hortense acted in the same noble way as her mother; never murmuring at the thought that the Imperial Crown might slip away from her remaining sons.

In 1813 she was ordered to go to Aix in Savoie to take the waters, and she reluctantly left her boys with her mother at Malmaison to be a comfort to her, though she could not bear to be separated from them.

Each place she went to seemed to have a tragedy in waiting for her, and Aix was no exception to this. One morning the queen, with Madame de Broc and others, arranged to have a picnic near the famous Cascade of Grésy, eight miles from Aix. About half a mile from it, the road being too bad to drive farther, they got out of the carriages and proceeded on foot to the cascade. To view it well it was necessary to cross the rapid and deep stream it fell into, on a narrow and rather rickety plank of wood. The queen, with the lightness of a sylph, ran across it swiftly, but, alas, Madame de Broc in following her slipped, fell, and disappeared into the torrent. The queen, alone on the other side, shrieked wildly, and while the others rushed to a mill close by for help, tore the shawl off her shoulders and threw the end into the stream, calling to her who no longer heard, to clutch hold of it. Many came to help and implored the queen to go away while they searched for her dearest friend. "No," she replied. "I will not leave this spot till her body is found," and, sitting down at the foot of a tree, holding her head in her hands, having no longer any strength or hope, kept repeating, weeping bitterly: "My God, what have I done that you treat me so cruelly? Was I not unhappy enough already?"

After a long search and with great effort the poor lady's body was found, but the force of the current was so great, and the bed of the river so full of jagged rocks, she was hardly recognisable. No words can depict the queen's grief, and for many days she could neither eat nor sleep. The thought of her children and her mother alone gave her strength to once again take up her duties and occupations, and she found some comfort in her sorrow in building and endowing a hospital for the poor of Aix, to be dedicated to the memory of her beloved friend.

In 1814, when France was in danger from the approach of the allied troops, she rejoined her mother in Paris. While here Mme. de

C—— begged her interest for one of her nephews who had been dismissed from the *Garde d'Honneur*, and was sentenced to death for having been concerned in an attempt on the life of M. Philippe de Segur, his colonel. This young officer owed it to the queen that he was not shot, as an able lawyer engaged by her was able to prove his innocence.

There is no sight that saddens, and at the same time invigorates and stirs up a nation more, than to see the Fatherland invaded. No one suffered with a heart more French than Hortense, nor bore her misfortunes with greater fortitude, which won for her the admiration and respect of the Allies.

On March 28th, 1814, Marshal Ney went to her house in the Rue Cerutti, to take her to the Tuileries for an interview with her sister-in-law, Marie Louise. She returned with an expression on her face which no one had ever before seen, and exclaimed to her ladies: "Oh, the cowardice and the treachery of which I have been witness. Can you believe it? She is leaving. She will ruin France and the emperor. Oh, in great trials it is the woman who should give an example of courage when the destinies of a country depend on her, also is it not her duty to defend the high position in which she has been placed?"

The queen then related to them her interview with Marie Louise. Hortense began the conversation by saying: "My sister, you ought not to leave Paris, as in doing so you neutralise its defence, and will eventually lose your crown and ours. I perceive that you are preparing to make this sacrifice with wonderful resignation."

The empress replied: "You are quite right, but it is not my fault. The council and the chancellor say it is impossible for me to refuse to do as they tell me."

On April 2nd, Josephine and Hortense both received an invitation from the Emperor Alexander of Austria to pay him a visit at Malmaison, unless they preferred that he should visit them. This request from the emperor was as flattering as it was delicate. He was moved to act thus by all the praises he had heard of these princesses, and evidently was as anxious to know them personally as to protect them. Hortense refused. Marie Louise had been sent to Rambouillet, where she was kept almost a prisoner, and she implored Hortense to go and stay with her. Hortense found two duties facing her, one that of remaining with her mother, the other of staying with the empress whom she could not but pity. Between two duties it is not always easy to select the right one, but after much consideration she decided to go to the empress, remembering she was suffering in a foreign country. She remained at Rambouillet till the Emperor of Austria decided that his daughter should return to Vienna. Hortense then returned to her mother to comfort her in her grief at the misfortunes of Napoleon.

The Allied Sovereigns were so struck by the noble conduct of Josephine's daughter, and their interest in her was so great, that they wished to separate her from her husband's family, and to give her sufficient income to secure her independence, but she refused, not wishing, as she said, to lose the privilege of being as unhappy as the others. What motive then induced her later on to accept the fortune assigned to her by the Treaty of Fontainebleau and the title of Duchess of St. Leu? It could only be from love of her children, and the thought of their future, a reason which would be an excuse for any mother, especially as they had been disinherited by the same treaty.

A fresh and terrible sorrow was still in store for her. When fate strikes one blow, it often has a second in reserve. Her mother died on May 19th, 1814. This loss deprived her not only of a loving mother, but of her best adviser. She might still have had some happiness if only all those she had made happy, and who owed many benefits to her, had been satisfied with forgetting her, but many of them turned into bitter enemies, accusing her of being an intriguer and a guilty person. As for her, the more ingratitude she received the less did she wish to seem ungrateful.

Feeling she ought to thank Louis XVIII for his arrangements for her future, she made him a visit of etiquette at the end of her mourning. The king received her very well and greatly praised her before the ladies of the new court. These would have passed over a simple reception, but they could not forgive the praise. They deemed the Duchesse de St. Leu as being the promoter of all the discontent, which later on resulted in the return of Napoleon from the Island of Elba. Thus are false accusations made.

On the evening of March 19th, 1815, one of the queen's ladies handed her a letter sent by Fouché by special messenger. The queen's eyes shone with terror when she read it, as it gave her information that a plot had been formed among the *Chouans* to disguise themselves in the uniform of the Imperial Guard and to waylay Napoleon on his way through France and assassinate him. "Great God, is it possible!" she exclaimed, thunderstruck. "But how to warn the emperor! Where is the man to be found to sacrifice himself. Anyone found with a letter of warning in his possession would be shot—unless Vincent (one of

The Duc de Berri

the queen's valets) would take the risk."

She quickly summoned him and placed the position clearly before him. He did not hesitate for a minute, and eagerly undertook the mission, full of pride at being able to endanger his life for his emperor. "Haste without delay," said Hortense, handing him Fouché's letter and a well-filled purse. "Take one of my horses and do not lose a moment."

Carefully hiding the precious letter in one of his boots and the purse in an inside pocket, and armed with pistols, he rode away within an hour, riding as much as possible through by-lanes and sleeping in his clothes at the poorest pot-houses. Once he was stopped at Villejuif by the Duc de Berri's troop, but, finding no reason for detaining him, as he made himself out as being a simple adventurer making his way to Africa, they let him proceed on his way. As he approached Essoune, where he heard Napoleon had halted, he could only ride slowly, as the roads were blocked by people assembling from all parts to greet their emperor. On approaching the town he saw a carriage driving towards him, escorted by a troop of lancers, and the Grand Maréchal, General Drouet, and the Duc de Vicenza riding by its side, and he had no difficulty in recognising his beloved master sitting with his arms crossed with an *aide-de-amp* next him. Vincent held up his hand and gave a military salute. The carriage stopped, and General Drouet rode up to him and asked what he wanted.

"To hand an important letter to His Majesty," he replied.

The emperor then said, "Who from?"

"Sire, it was entrusted to me to give to Your Majesty by the Queen of Holland."

"Ah, the poor Hortense. Is she well?"

"Yes, sire."

"Is Paris quiet?"

"Yes, sire."

"Well, we shall soon see this for ourselves."

He read the letter silently, and handed it to General Drouet, bidding him see to it, and to take all precautions; then, having handed a purse to Vincent, he ordered the cavalcade to move on, amid the acclamations of the population. Vincent returned to Paris as quickly as he could and gave a full account of all to Hortense.

As soon as the emperor arrived in Paris, Hortense, accompanied by her sister-in-law Queen Julie, went to the Tuileries and made their way through the large apartments with great difficulty (so crowded were they by the people who had been allowed in to see the emperor) to Napoleon's private rooms. Hortense fell at his knees and could not speak from shedding tears of joy. Napoleon gently lifted her up, embraced her affectionately, and asked where her children were.

"Sire, they are in safety."

"*Madame*," he continued, calmly, though himself deeply touched, "you have placed my nephews in a false position, in the midst of my enemies. I want to see your brother; I wrote to him from Lyons. And your suit with Louis, how is it going on?"

"Ah, sire," the queen replied, "Your Majesty's return will win it for me."

The Bourbons had fled precipitately from Paris the night before Napoleon's return, with the exception of the Duchesse de Bourbon and the Duchesse d'Orleans, mother of Louis Philippe, who had broken her leg a few days before. She informed Hortense of her state of suffering. Immediately the queen replied that she would be happy to take her under her protection, and the following day again went to the Tuileries and interceded for the *duchesse*, and did not leave the emperor till he gave his consent for her to remain in Paris and to be treated in the way due to her rank, and not to move before the doctor allowed her to do so. A similar privilege was accorded to the Duchesse de Bourbon, and as Napoleon never did things by halves, he allotted to the Duchesse d'Orléans an income of 500,000 *francs* and to the Duchesse de Bourbon a pension of 250,000.

Alas, Napoleon's ill-fortune once more overtook him. Again he rode at the head of his beloved army, but no longer to lead it to victory, but to sore defeat. The bad news which came daily to Paris saddened all, culminating as it did in that of the disastrous Battle of Waterloo. The population still hoped against hope, and it was not until Napoleon's sad return to Paris that it was realised that all was lost.

Hortense left Malmaison, never to see it again. She was only allowed twenty-four hours to pack up and be out of French territory. Before leaving, she sent a farewell letter to the emperor, begging him to accept the one article of value she possessed, a pearl necklace valued at 200,000 *francs*, the one which Napoleon, when he arrived at St. Helena, entrusted to M. de Las Casas' care, lest it might be taken from him as had been the case with his money.

Hortense decided on making her home in Switzerland, but on arriving at Geneva the authorities would not allow her to remain there. She then thought of the hospice she had founded at Aix. Here she was well received, and decided to remain there with her sons till she knew the final decision of the allies with regard to her. One of her sons had soon to leave her, as King Louis sent an order for him to join him in Italy. She soon retired to a modest retreat at Arenenberg, on the Lake of Constance, the Swiss Government having granted her permission to do so, and here she lived quietly with her other son and a few friends who remained faithful to her. In the evenings she invited some of her neighbours to come and talk over all the glorious, but sad past, which already began to assume the vast proportions which history has since given it.

The eldest son of the queen, Napoleon Louis, who had been sent for by his father, married his cousin, a daughter of King Joseph, and lived at Florence. He was full of zeal and eager to devote himself to the happiness of others. In spite of all the grandeur he had been surrounded with since his childhood, and which his mother feared might have a bad influence on him, he remained unselfish, and simple in his way of life, and adopted the principle she had strongly engrafted in him: "That one must be a man before being a prince," also, "That rise in rank is only one more obligation towards others, and that misfortune, if it comes, met bravely, gives birth to nobler qualities."

His brother, Louis Napoleon, had the same sentiments and the same characteristics; he had but one desire, to return to France. His eyes were always turned towards his Fatherland, which he loved, and he occupied his mind with the thoughts of all that he would do for its happiness and glory. Till then his one ambition was to fight for France in the ranks, but in 1830, the glorious days of Italy's awakening filled both the brothers' hearts with enthusiasm and sympathy. Louis had been well trained in the military schools of France, and he and his brother were the first to take up arms and join as volunteers in the ranks of the Italian patriots. The queen, devoured by anxiety, went precipitately to Italy, with only one idea, to be near her sons.

What was her horror to hear at each halt: "Napoleon killed!— Napoleon killed!" She heard, but did not believe. When she arrived at Pesaro she was met by her youngest son, Louis, who in floods of tears clasped her in his arms, saying, "You are all that is left to me in the world." Hortense fainted, and it was many days before she became calm enough for the doctor to tell her of a fresh anxiety, which was that it was imperative for Louis to go at once to Paris to be treated by one of the best doctors there for an internal disorder causing him great pain, and which he was trying to hide from his mother.

This roused her from her grief and all her thoughts turned to him. She at once arranged to start off immediately, and if not allowed to stay in Paris (as the decree of banishment had not been reversed), to cross to England. Louis tenderly embraced her, and said: "My mother, let us start at once. If I am to die, let it be in France. At least I shall now have the joy of seeing my country once more."

They started. All was made easy for them. On arriving in Paris she sent for the doctor and wrote to M. d'Houdetot, the king's *aide-de-camp*, to announce her arrival. She was lodged a few steps from the Place Vendôme. It was May 5th, the anniversary of Napoleon's death. An immense crowd had assembled; hymns were sung, and crosses of immortelles and laurels were placed at the foot of the column. Hortense could not resist the force of recollection, and notwithstanding her strict *incognito*, she stood for a moment on the balcony fancying herself once more in the glorious Empire days when joyful Parisians were celebrating some new victory. The reality soon returned to her, and she shed bitter tears.

M. d'Houdetot came to see the queen the next day, and told her that the king, to whom she had also written to ask for permission to remain some days in Paris, could not do so without referring the matter to his "responsible ministers," and that in consequence M. Casimir Perrier would call and see her. He called the same day, and after a long conversation the queen said, "I know well I am transgressing the law. I have weighed all its consequences, and you have the right to arrest me; it would only be just."

The minister interrupted her, saying: "Just, no; legal, yes."

However, he gave her permission to see the king himself. The next day M. d'Houdetot took her to the Tuileries, and the king gave her a kind reception and asked much after her son and her family, and said:

"I know, and feel deeply for all your sorrows, and if it had depended only on me, I would have saved you from them. I also know you have legitimate reclamations to make, which you have made in vain to former ministers. Write me a line to say all that is due to you; I know how to manage affairs and will take charge of yours."

Then, asking if she would like to see his wife and sister, he went to fetch them.

A few days afterwards the council decided that the queen might go to London as soon as her son could travel. He had obtained great relief from the doctor, and soon was out of danger. A further favour the queen asked from M. Casimir Perrier was, that when she left England she might be allowed to go to Vichy for the waters, which she had asked for before, but had been denied, as she was told that her presence there might lead to an outbreak in favour of Napoleon, she being his stepdaughter, and he having been so popular in that district. Casimir said it would be better for her to write from England and ask for this permission, as coming from English doctors, and he added: "As to yourself personally, the people little by little will get accustomed to see you, but as regards your son, his name would be an obstacle; he would have to change it. We are obliged to study the foreign powers, and we have so many parties in France, war would be fatal to us."

When the queen repeated this conversation to her son, he made a great effort to lift himself up from his bed, and cried, "Give up my name, I—and they dared to make you such a proposition—no, never! Let us return to our quiet retreat, which you chose so well, my mother."

Some days afterwards they crossed to England, where her son recuperated for three months, and then started back for Arenenberg without passing through France. After three years of peace, Hortense's health visibly began to decline, and symptoms of the cruel illness which was to bring her to the tomb showed themselves. Her son had joined the army, and when the outbreak at Strasburg took place, she heard rumours through the newspapers that her son had been arrested. Ill as she was, in great haste she travelled in strict *incognito* and went to Virey to the Duchesse de Raguse, her friend, in order to be able to intercede for the prince, but no sooner had she got there than she was ordered to leave immediately, though her companion, Madame de Faverolles, represented to M. Molé, the president, that grave anxiety and the fatigue of a journey so rapidly undertaken had caused her violent suffering, ill as she was, and that the queen required immediate attendance from doctors, and at least a few days' rest. All was of no avail, and she was ordered to leave at once. This culminated her illness, and her malady took such a violent character that the skill of the doctors was of no avail, and she breathed her last on October 5th, 1837.

Simple in the midst of glory; courageous in the midst of adversities; ever unselfish and merciful, Hortense can today render to God a good account of her short-lived prosperity, of which she only let others profit. France she ever loved and ever wept for. She was a devoted mother and daughter, and would have been a devoted wife if circumstances had been different. After her family, what she valued beyond a crown and grandeur was "friends."

Canonnier à pied et Officier d'artillerie légère

GARDE IMPÉRIALE.

Gardes d'honneur (sous-officier), tenue de campagne, et Éclaireurs

GARDE IMPÉRIALE.

Chapter 2

A First Love

Napoleon was by no means perfect. General M——, who had known him from boyhood, during one of the many conversations I had with him, said:

"Napoleon's faults never rose from viciousness, but through want of self-control, and his ideas were always noble and generous. His sobriety was so remarkable that he often had to endure the ridicule of his comrades. Though not of a character to wish to quarrel, he at first quietly defended himself; but when their attacks became too virulent, his penetrating look and the cold smile which spread over his features warned his tormentors that he would no longer allow himself to be a target, even to those older than himself and in a higher position in life than he was. He loved abstract studies. His favourite authors were those who gave him food for reflection, and if he wanted relaxation, he read Ossian, Shakespeare, etc. His words were few and often sarcastic. He detested affectation of any kind, and liked people to speak frankly and openly to him.

"What he had to say was always said briefly and clearly. Whatever he had to write, even his love letters, were written in a small space and as concise as possible. He could express more in a single line than others in a whole page. Napoleon was a dreamer, and often a romantic one. I have seen him raise up his eyes to the skies for a long time in deep thought at the close of a beautiful day in Italy. This man, whose mind was so occupied by thoughts of ambition and power, nevertheless had depths of deep and passionate affection in his nature. This even lasted a long time after his marriage. I have seen him at night, before going to bed, take the portrait of his wife with him, a habit he still kept up after he was emperor. He always confessed that his heart beat with emotion if he perceived in the distance the white dress of a young woman appearing through the trees.

"He often stopped in the dark alleys of the park at Malmaison to listen to the soft pealing of the village bells for Vespers at the small village of Ruel. Yet Napoleon has been accused of having no religious principles, and of being a comedian when he attended religious ceremonies. He despised atheists and the women who did not pray. He said 'that Italian women prayed to God for forgiveness when they erred,' and had at least that advantage over the French, adding, 'A woman without remorse is a most sad and pitiable conquest.'

"Among the characteristic traits which I can cite of Napoleon, I will relate you one which lives in my memory, and proves his extreme delicacy of feelings towards women. When he was commander in the artillery at Toulon, I was his sub-officer. We were very intimate. Often he talked to me frankly of his affairs, including his love episodes. 'You,' he said, to me one day, 'succeed to a fortune, so do not mind wasting it on a woman. You are their slave; they lead you like a child. As for me, I revere them, I adore them; they strongly excite my imagination, but I have a sufficiently just idea of their moral organisation not to allow myself to be ruled by *them*. I have *there* (striking his forehead) that which occupies me more than anything else.'

"All the same. Napoleon was so constituted that he could not resist the fascination of women, and therefore I was not surprised when one evening he stopped in front of me saying, in an abrupt manner, 'Louis, decidedly I am in love.'

"'In love with whom?' I exclaimed.

"'With a young girl who lives in a little house beyond the ramparts. She has nothing but her beauty, and is really charming; moreover, she possesses a refined mind and a gentle manner. I spend hours looking into her beautiful blue eyes and admiring her slender and graceful figure.'

"'And no doubt she loves you?'

"'Yes, just a little, in Italian childish fashion, not like a woman of the world, who makes sure that her hair is well done before she looks at you tenderly.'

"'Well,' I replied laughingly, 'she must be a charming companion for you.'

"'Yes, but this girl has a mother, an Italian, a widow, whom I greatly respect . Her husband, who was of a good family, sacrificed everything to marry her, as this lady's virtue was unassailable; but, alas! the poor man died two years after the marriage, from illness brought on by hard work and anxiety, leaving his wife with a daughter, and penniless. She has worked hard for her livelihood by taking in needlework, and has brought up her child to be honest and virtuous, and in the present case she shows her trust in her, by having confidence in my loyalty. However, the other evening, after sending her daughter away, she said, "Monsieur Bonaparte, you love Naddi! You must not come here any more, or you must swear to me on your sword that you will respect my beloved child, and not take the least advantage of her innocence. In short, that you will not lead her to any step which might cause her to forget her duty to, or separate her from me. Her only fortune is the work of my hands, and her own, which are still unskilled. I swore to her father, who died from his honest love of me, that so long as I lived, I would guard her from all evil. Believe me, this (bringing out an Italian stiletto from her pocket) would prove to her as well as to you what would be the result if she forgot herself. I must forbid any further visit unless you take the oath which I demand. Will you swear?"

"'"I will take the oath," I replied, "and indeed I will neither see Naddi again nor speak to her, without your permission." And this promise I have kept,' he continued, 'But, oh, I am very unhappy.'

"'How did you get to know these ladies' I asked him.

"'Their house was going to be demolished—that is to say, those gentlemen "geniuses" who wish to destroy all old buildings had decided on this. I was charged to see to it, and I found that the little dwelling did not in the least hinder our operations. The commission gave me an introduction to these ladies, and this is the consequence.'

"For several days the commander was anxious-looking and sorrowful. At last he asked me what I thought of a love marriage.

"'That depends,' I said; 'for a man who has no ambition it is often a happy destiny, but one who has a future before him should never make a love marriage; to do it is to paralyse his existence and to bar the road to fortune.'

"'That is true,' said he—'that is true; you are right, my dear Louis.'

"Two days passed without my seeing Napoleon; on the third, he wrote me a little note, more legible than usual, to ask me to come and see him, because he was ill.

"I went, and found him sitting with a large coffee-pot beside him, out of which he filled a cup every quarter of an hour. I remarked that this diet was far from being good for his indisposition.

"'I have a report to make this evening,' he said to me; 'I must clear my head, and when I am in a bad humour coffee puts me right.'

"'Is there something wrong with your love affair?'

"'On the contrary,' he replied, 'it was almost going too well, but happily I was able to restrain myself.'

"I looked at him with a curiosity which he understood, for he said at once:

"'I do not like to speak much of myself, and especially of things which men regard as childish, still I feel the necessity of telling you what has happened, for I am really sorry. The day before yesterday, I arrived at the widow's house. She had gone out, but Naddi was there, beautiful and charming as usual. For a good while I kept answering in the coldest possible way her innocent teasings; but she began to cry, and to reproach me for my coldness. I wished to reassure her, to comfort her, and I found myself so near that danger was imminent. Naddi cried, gently leaning on my arm. I consoled her as well as I could, without knowing exactly what I was saying. I promised her many things, I even went so far as to engage myself, when Naddi, half overcome, pushed me gently back, and, seizing the hilt of my sword, asked me to swear on it that I would be her husband. Then a cold shiver went through me, and happily for her, and above all for myself, I had the power to remain an honourable man, telling her that I could not take such an oath. These women,' continued Napoleon, 'nothing stops them when they are in love. In spite of my refusal, Naddi became still more tender. I freed myself from her arms, and had the courage to leave her.

"'A little way from the house I met her mother, to whom I told everything. She thanked me cordially, but begged me to abstain altogether from seeing her daughter. "But," she continued, "my poor child will be very unhappy. If I could return to Florence, the distraction of the journey and the absence would perhaps cure her; here she passes a sad life, and I am so ill and—"

"'"If you wish to give me a proof of your regard," I said, "accept from me what you require to return to your home. Do not forget me, and do not tell Naddi to forget me altogether." . . .

"'If you had seen, Louis, how she held my hands. . . . And this morning I have sent her three months of my allowance, which I have borrowed, without knowing how to return it; but—we shall see. From now till then many things may take place; however this may be, Naddi has made me pass moments as happy as those I passed with Adelaide, seven years ago, when I was in the garrison at Valencia.'

"'Who was Adelaide?' I asked him; 'you have never spoken to me of her.'

"'She was the daughter of a Madame de Colombier,' Napoleon replied, with a great sigh; 'I went to spend all my free evenings at her house. Her daughter and I could not have been more innocent. Imagine, we arranged little rendezvous in the middle of summer at dawn, and, you will hardly believe it, all our happiness consisted in eating cherries together.'

"Here I interrupted the commander with a great burst of laughter. Napoleon shrugged his shoulders, and looked at me with a smile of sarcasm.

"'My dear Louis,' he said, 'the human race possesses two great virtues which one cannot respect too highly—courage in man and modesty in woman.' He then took another cup of coffee and bade me goodbye.

"This man, who at the same time acted with so much generosity and gentleness, he who spoke so wisely, was then without any fortune, and almost in need! Soon after he commanded armies and sat on a throne, which he raised above all the thrones of Europe. One day in the Tuileries I dared to recall to the emperor the memory of Naddi.

"'Ah, my dear fellow,' he replied, 'do not speak of that; that is one of the most real and most sincere love affairs which I have had in my life, but then I was only a poor commander in the artillery.'

"Since then Napoleon loved many others, but as a despot, breaking and mastering women's hearts.

"Having become more powerful and, above all, richer than he was at Toulon, he lost his good faith in love and his delicacy of feeling so rare and so pure, though he still had moments of trust, no less beautiful and no less sublime.

"I shall speak of that another time, for I love to talk of my emperor, of my hero, of this wonderful being, of this great genius, who in one word understood everything, and who enveloped the world at a glance."

This was the tale of General M———.

Bonaparte, premier consul).

A MARENGO.

Trompette des Dragons de l'Impératrice, et Timbalier des Chevau-légers lanciers.

GARDE IMPÉRIALE.

CHAPTER 3

Hébert

What I am going to relate is not a made-up story; it is a perfectly true biography of a man I knew, and who himself told me all these events in his life. I made notes of them at the time, and have put them together to make the story as concise as possible.

1

For several months the year '89 had let loose its passions; three assemblies and a monarchy had been engulfed in the revolutionary abyss. In the interests of France, fearful and terrible scenes were taking place, and a suspended sword hung over the heads of the populace. The Directory continued the Convention which it had denounced, but the country, no longer concurring in its tyrannical measures, now joined in the fanatical cry for liberty. It had lost all faith in its rulers, and only feared them. Beyond it France could cast with pride the tired gaze of her eyes on the young and most noble of her children. Fourteen armies, drawn from the Mother country, were opposed as young soldiers against old armies in Europe. There, needless to say, generous blood flowed, but it flowed for its country and not for the scaffold.

All these regiments, officers and soldiers, were principally composed of volunteers and adventurers, and among them was the obscure young man who gives the name to this story, Hébert, who at the first cry, "To arms!" "To the frontier!" made his way to join one of the regiments of the First Army, which was ordered to Italy, where it remained for three years in the Alps under the Generals Dumerbion, Kellerman, and Scherer. Proud indeed he was when he made one of the volunteers from Dijon, beating his drum so violently that he stunned the ears of his companions the whole way from the town till they reached the headquarters of the Army of the Alps.

Truth to say, his enthusiasm for soldiering rather cooled down during his first year spent in the mountains; the cold was great and privations were many, but he was brave and industrious, and also was gifted with a cheerful spirit. He made his comrades dance to the music of his flute, and he taught them to play on it, which they did better than himself, and he then joined in the dance. He was the barber of his regiment as well as being a music-master. Gold and silver were not common in the army of the Alps, and notes of hand were not accepted. But as Hébert had read that in primitive days when money did not exist people did all their commerce by exchange, he applied this system of the ancient times to a later civilisation. Therefore, he willingly taught a dance step in exchange for a glass of brandy, and he shaved his comrades for a week in exchange for bread for the same period.

However, this way of trading was very nearly fatal to him, for he was very near being shot as a thief. One day an adjutant in a bad temper, going his rounds, found a chicken in his bag. In vain Hébert declared he had been given this innocent fowl by a passing comrade whom he had taught a Basque dance. The adjutant would not listen, and, pointing his gun at poor, trembling Hébert, said he would take him to the colonel, who would have him court-martialled and shot, if he did not give the bird up, which Hébert did like lightning, and later on had the sad satisfaction of seeing his adjutant enjoying the good meal to which he had been looking forward.

Hébert took his soldiering earnestly, but he admitted that when he was lighting on the heights, burned by the hot sun during the day and frozen by the east night winds, he cried out more than once, "Goodness gracious! Glory may be superb, but all the same it is tiresome." This was certainly a barbarism, if not blasphemy, from a warlike point of view, but we must remember that when the poor recruit cried:

"Long live the Fatherland!" "To arms for the Fatherland!" he did not understand all it meant, and his intelligence did not grasp fully for whom and for what aim he was lighting. The moment, however, was not far off when he would find one in whom his existence would be fused, and to whom his whole life would be devoted; in short, "Saïd was to find his Mahomet."

2

Towards the month of March, 1796, the army which seemed to have been almost forgotten among the rocks of Liguria, was led by a young Corsican, who had been appointed general of one division in place of the incompetent Scherer. Nothing from the exterior of the young general appealed to the eye at first sight; he was short, had dark hair and complexion, and was very stout, with penetrating eyes; his smile was cold and sarcastic; he looked delicate and lymphatic; his white and well-cared for hands did not seem fitted for hard work. A stranger would, therefore, have been surprised that the *Directoire*, who had men in their pay of Herculean strength, equal to their courage, should have selected to strengthen the moral of their army, which was without bread and munitions, a little Corsican, whose frail appearance did not look as if he would be able to survive two nights of open-air bivouac; but the moment this man cast his scrutinising glance on the sad but brave remnants of the Italian army, the soldiers made the air resound and the rocks re-echo with shouts of "*Vive le General Bonaparte!*" showing how in one moment they had fallen under his magnetic power.

Besides this, in their new general many recognised "*le Petit Caporal*," who had won all their hearts by his devotion to the army and zeal for his work, also by being a true and faithful friend, ever ready to help any of his comrades who got into trouble, by shifting the fault from their shoulders to his, if possible. Napoleon, now in command, became their idol. Like magic, ragged uniforms were repaired and smartened up, the soldiers all vying with each other in extra permissible adornments. Hébert's company was remarkable for the coquettishness of its pig-tails and beards. Bonaparte, whose eagle eye nothing escaped, showed a visible satisfaction in seeing these adornments. The discouraged Hébert had become "a man and true soldier" again; his "*sous*" were very few, but he found ways of smartening himself.

Dignified and simple words were addressed by Napoleon to the troops, words of which he already knew the effect. He bestowed high praise on the fragments of the repaired uniforms, and pointed out how much honour was woven in them.

Hébert, the barber soldier, appropriated these compliments to himself, and, quite forgetting he was not allowed to speak from the ranks, took the liberty of exclaiming loudly, "Well, this is a general who understands things properly, and whoever has the honour of being his hairdresser is indeed a lucky fellow." Napoleon smiled and looked fixedly at the young recruit, but he did not ask his name. He may, perhaps, have thought for a moment of granting the young man's wishes, but this post was already in the hands of an old servant he greatly loved, so he passed silently on. "I am a fool," said Hébert, and his spirits sank, thinking of the reprimand and punishment which might await him for having called out as he had done. However, his buoyancy soon returned, and when the company was ordered to break up and disperse, no one obeyed with such alacrity as Hébert, and, once his gun was laid aside, he displayed his happiness by making pirouettes and going head over heels for the amusement of his comrades till his hilarity worked itself off.

"Imagine," said Hébert, when he was telling me this part of his life—"imagine that within a fortnight of his arrival, 'le Petit Caporal,' how, I knew not, had transplanted us into the fields of Italy, and we found ourselves in the rear of the Austrians, and, oh, our pride! We all had new uniforms, new plumes in our casques, silver in our pockets; we consumed rice and macaroni, and, I must add, that the Italian women were not so shy as those in the mountains." We now arrived at the point when the Great Man and the obscure one were to become acquainted.

3

After the battles of Roveredo, Bassano, and St. Georges, all of which Napoleon had won for France, while Marmont went to Paris to lay the captured flags of the enemy at the feet of the *Directoire*, the army rested for a while, within easy reach of Milan, where Bonaparte relaxed his mind from the fatigues of wax by superintending administrative works for the benefit of the town and country which became imperishable monuments. At the same time he did not neglect his army, and few days passed without his riding through the camps to cast a master's eye on them. Some of each raiment were billeted in the small towns, others in villages and in wooden huts built by the soldiers themselves, and these were cleverly decorated, according to the talent of the builder, with paintings of all kinds. Shops, *cafés*, and small theatres grew up, and each had their signboard hanging over the doors, with quaint and fantastic devices on them; names were borrowed from Paris for the different quarters of the camp, such as the "*Boulevard du Temple,*" "*le Champs Elysées,*" "*la Palais Royal,*" etc.

During one of his rides through the camp, so animated and so various, Napoleon could not fail to notice one special shop from the extraordinary painting which adorned its wooden frontage. It consisted of a most weird violet-blue sky, on which the artist had ingeniously fixed large gilded stars cut out in cardboard; the door was painted a darker blue, with silver stars sprinkled over it; and above the door, in large silver letters, was written, "A razor of honour—Barber and Hairdresser, Hébert," and hanging from a nail, tied on by tri-colour riband, hung a large razor. The general on reading this inscription was puzzled, and determined to find out its meaning.

Bonaparte had, since he was made general, instituted a new reward, that of awarding to any soldier who had performed a special act of bravery a sword or pistol, and he knew that his enemies had turned this practice into ridicule, and even Moreau had made fun of it by presenting to his cook "A sauce-pan of honour" as a reward, and he feared that there might be some analogy between this fact which had been reported to him and the inscription which he had before his eyes, and he sent his *aide-de-camp* to order the proprietor of the hut to come out and speak to him.

The trembling Hébert approached, and to the sharp demand of the general, "Your name?" he replied.

"Hébert, the same as my father and mother."

"Were you ever in the army of the Rhine?"

"No, a volunteer in the army of Italy. I preferred that."

"Why have you dared to make fun of the reward I bestow on my brave soldiers, by putting up that absurd inscription and in painting your hut in that ridiculous fashion?"

"Citizen General, I swear to you by the firmament, which is the same colour as my hut, that if there is any fun-making in it, it is that of my comrades, and not mine."

"Explain yourself clearly, unless you prefer prison."

"I certainly prefer to explain myself. Some weeks ago we were still in the fighting; during a lull I was shaving, in the ambulance, a grenadier of the 32nd Brigade who had received a slight scratch at Lodi, but was going to rejoin the ranks. Of course he wanted to adorn himself for the fray, so as not to appear untidy in face of the enemy."

"Let us come to the real facts."

"Well, he was seated on a three-legged stool, as there were no chairs; I was making him look ten years younger, while the fight was going on some hundreds of yards from us."

"Shorten your story—shorten it!"

"I had already shaved one half of his face and was preparing to shave the other, when what should burst in front of us but a shell which covered us with dust from head to foot."

"The grenadier did not move, I suppose?"

"No, neither did I, Citizen General—that is to say, I did move on the contrary. 'Do not disturb yourself,' I said to the other, and then I went to the shell and pulled out its fuse and went back and finished my man without scratching him in the least. It is on account of this that my comrades have honoured me by decorating my hut as you see. This is the truth, Citizen General, and the whole truth, as sure as that you are '*le Petit Caporal.*'"

Bonaparte could hardly contain himself with delight, for he had found one of those men of iron by whom he liked to be surrounded, whatever rank or employment he might give them. Turning again to Hébert, he said: "You do not easily get into a fright, it appears?"

"You are right, my General."

"Well, you shall join me at Milan shortly."

So saying, Bonaparte rode away, having given directions to the colonel of the regiment to send Hébert to his palace at Milan on the following day, where he was to be his barber.

Who can describe Hébert's joy and elation. He rushed about among his comrades, crying, "Congratulate me!—Wish me joy! Share all my belongings, my money, sword and gun—yes, all except the 'razor of honour'? Look out for another barber. My occupation is now fixed. I am going to Milan. I shall shave '*le Petit Caporal.*' Hurrah for '*le Petit Caporal!*'" He then dragged many of his friends to the *café*, ordered bottles of wine, and made them all tipsy, including the grenadier of Lodi, and the following day, amid huzzas of his raiment, he departed for Milan on the back of an old horse hired for eight *francs*.

Hébert was lodged among the servants at the palace, and as soon as he had been suitably clothed *en bourgeois*, he began his duties, which he took most seriously. He was definitely appointed barber to his general, and later on he succeeded to being also his hairdresser, the old man having retired with a pension. His delight and pride were greater than ever. Unluckily, he did not leave any memoirs giving details of his life at Milan, but a few letters have been found which he wrote to his father at this date. The following extracts are a specimen:

From our Headquarters at Milan,
6th October, 1796.

My dear Father.

We have just sent off 12 millions again to those robbers of the *Directoire*. I send you at the same time three gold pieces, which I have saved from my wages.

10*th*.—I take the opportunity of large boxes of pictures by M.

Raphael and many other valuable articles being sent off to Paris to enclose you my portrait, also one of my hero, for whom I would lose my head—and my tail, if I had one. I profited by the drawing lessons you gave me to do his portrait myself, fixing his appearance in my mind while I was shaving him or doing his hair.

3rd November.—It appears that the Austrians have not yet had enough of our guns, as fighting is going to recommence, so, '*To horse!—to horse!*'

14th November,—All grows hotter, my dear father. General Vaubois is getting entangled; one can see that with one eye. Today I passed in terror, but understand, not for myself, but for him who is my second father, '*le Petit Caporal*,' who had two horses killed under him, the shells were whistling all round him while he remained perfectly calm.

In another letter he wrote:

At last we have signed the Treaty of Campo-Formio, You will soon hear of it, my father. We have signed the peace of Europe, and we are leaving for somewhere, I know not where, very early tomorrow, but I have orders to be ready at 1 a.m.

Hébert accompanied Napoleon first to Rastadt and then on to Paris, where they put up in the Rue Chantereine. In his leisure hours the valet hairdresser liked walking about the streets and *boulevards*—anywhere, in fact, where he could hear the praises of his beloved master. Certainly, if he had heard any citizen speak a word against him, he would never have done it twice. Fortunately, there was little danger of anything else, for never had popularity risen to a higher degree among all classes. No one could repress their admiration; the name of Napoleon became truly an object of national religion.

On returning to the *hôtel*, Hébert, as if still not being able to realise his happiness, kept saying to himself: "And it is I—I who have the honour of dressing that head. Is it not I must be dreaming? "It is certain that if any one had come from the Grand Turk, offering him hundreds of gold *ducats* to perform the same office for him, Hébert would have refused it with disdain. His hands must be kept pure from all other contact; he would not even use them to shave himself. He had his own barber.

4

"Land!—land!" shouted the sailors keeping watch on board the *Orient*, the *Franklin*, the *Peuple*, the *Souveraine*, the *Semiramis*, and the *Toussaint*, which vessels formed the advance guard of the French squadron. "Land!—land!" echoed from the crews of the *Spartiade*, the *Guillaume Tell*, the *Genereux*, and the *Justice*, etc., which ships formed the reserve. The inhabitants of Malta, to which island the fleet was approaching, must have been greatly astonished and alarmed to hear the roar of 30,000 voices, those of the victors of Arcola and Rivoli, shouting and singing the "*Marseillaise*" to the deafening accompaniment of drums and trumpets. The Italian army had become temporarily a navy, and "*Le Petit Caporal*" its High Admiral. The Knights of Jerusalem, from their rocks, waved large tricolour flags, and the so-called impregnable island surrendered to him.

A short stay was made at Malta, to land sufficient men to garrison it, and leaving a certain number of ships to guard the harbour. The remainder of the fleet spread their white sails and continued their dangerous voyage to Egypt, completely outwitting Nelson, who was on the look-out for them, and within a very short time Bonaparte, with his hand resting on *Kléber's* broad shoulder, landed on the soil of Egypt, the object of his ambitious dreams.

Hébert, as one can imagine, had followed his master without knowing or asking whither they were bound. He was always content and joyous if with him. His position had greatly improved, not only in point of money, but also with regard to his intercourse with Napoleon, who often when in a good humour had a talk with him. One day in public he pulled his ear, which was always a special sign of his favour. One of these conversations took place at Cairo, when Napoleon said:

"Well, Hébert, what do you think of this country?"

"Citizen General, I think it is fearfully hot, but as you must be as hot as I am, I do not complain."

"What about the Pyramids?"

"I think they are very useful to write our names on, as one does on the Belvedere in the Zoological Gardens in Paris."

"And what about the inhabitants?"

"I think they have not enough hair on their heads and too much beard."

"And the Mamelukes?"

"Excuse me, general, but I cannot express my opinion of them, owing to the fact of your having taken one into your service—that rogue of a little Arab called Roustan."

"Silence, Hébert, you are jealous; that is not right. It is an experiment. The Mamelukes are fine horsemen. I am going to have a regiment of them. They will make a fine effect in France."

Hébert never uttered a word, carefully cleaned his precious razors, and laid them in a vermilion leather case on which the initials of Josephine Beauharnais were engraved, and, having finished his duties, he respectfully withdrew. But his expression had changed, for it was never without an inward rage that he spoke or thought of Roustan. He was an object of antipathy and hatred to him. On going out he found the Mameluke lying across the door on a lion-skin rug. For a moment he felt inclined to give him a good kick, but restrained himself, and gave him a scowling stare which Roustan returned.

Egypt was hard for Bonaparte's soldiers, hard for sailors, hard for all the brave sons of France, who cried in vain for "*la Patrie*" amid its terrible deserts. All suffered and many died from the poisonous winds of Jaffa, generals and men, the doctors and patients, the enemy and the invader, a terrible equality of death, which was to be renewed twelve years later on the ice and snow-clad fields of Russia. During these hard times Hébert would never acknowledge he was ill, although blood ran out of his eyes and his mouth was parched and dry from the sand he swallowed in crossing the desert. All his thoughts were for his general, and his love for him redoubled at every step.

One evening, when after a painful burning march he and many others were deceived by a mirage, representing on the far horizon smiling green fields, trees and water, he jumped for joy, laughing and clapping his hands like a child, exclaiming: "Oh, how my general will enjoy sweet rest under those shady trees! How *we* shall enjoy bathing in the water!" Bitterly he and all wept when they found it was only a deception! Ere long, his constitution was no proof against the plague, but neither this, from which Desgenettes, the doctor, saved him, nor a wound from a Turkish bullet which broke his jaw at St. Jean d'Acre, drew a tear or murmur from him, but on his recovery a grief more terrible than anything he had experienced tore his heart asunder.

On being informed that his general during his illness had embarked for France with Berthier, Lannes, Marmont and Murat, and—oh! this was the cruellest blow of all—and Roustan, "Alas!" cried Hébert, "through my illness I have been left behind." It was some consolation to him to find that Napoleon had left special orders for him to be well cared for. All the same, for the first time in his life he wept bitterly, his mind nearly gave way, his wound reopened, and he had another long and dangerous illness. When he finally recovered. General Kléber, to whose care Napoleon had confided him, said he would attach him to his service.

"You are very good, general," Hébert replied, with a melancholy look, half comic and half touching. "I will gladly accept and will do my best. You have certainly very beautiful hair, but it is not the same as his!" And every day, with his eyes fixed on the shore, he asked, "When, oh when, will a ship sail for Europe?"

5

"*Halte la !—halte la!—halte la!*" was the cry from a sentry, and no answer being given, it was followed by shots and a call to arms, and a few minutes after the aggressor, the man whom the shots had not touched, was made a prisoner by a strong escort, and brought before the Austrian commander.

The man had been seized just as he was attempting to swim across a river close to the camp. His attire could not indeed inspire confidence. He was shoeless and in rags, and it was not surprising that the Austrian officer, to whom he was conducted, thought him a spy, and his questions were neither easy nor polite. Who are you?"

Once I was somebody, now I am nobody."

"Where do you come from?"

"From Egypt, without stopping."

"You are telling a lie, and want to deceive me."

"I have never told a lie. *Once* a man accused me of telling one; he never did so again. I gave him a lesson he will never forget."

"Ah, you have audacity and courage; all the better for you, for you will need it. Where were you going when we caught you?"

"To the headquarters of the French Army."

"As a soldier?"

"No, not as a soldier."

"Then probably it was to describe all you see in our lines and to report all you hear—you are risking your life for gold *louis*, but I can tell you you have lost your game."

"You imply that *I*—I am a spy?" And a blush of shame spread over the poor man's face. "Commander," he added, "you have no right to insult a prisoner."

"Well, well, reply frankly. If you are not a soldier or a spy, what were you going to do at the headquarters of the French Army?"

"What no one among you has ever done—I was going to return to the First Consul to dress his hair."

At this reply the commander lifted his sword as if to strike Hébert, but looking at his angry countenance, restrained from doing so and instead called to his men to put him under arrest till it could be ascertained whether he was a spy, in which case he would be shot. He then took out his pipe to smoke. Hébert felt his last hour was come, and kept repeating to himself, "Now I shall never see my master again—never, never again," when, hark, what was that roar he heard in the distance! He knew not, but the general did, for suddenly the cry ran through the camp, "To arms!—to arms!" and in the confusion he was set free, and found himself in the midst of a battle. General Gaudine having fallen on the Austrians unexpectedly with a detachment of artillery.

The attack was quite unexpected, and shells were falling thick all round him. How Hébert escaped he knew not—indeed, he had no recollection of anything until two days afterwards when he found himself in a tent surrounded by French soldiers. He gazed on them with astonishment. "Yes, yes, *mon brave*," said one of them, lifting up his head to pour some brandy down his throat, "you have had a narrow squeak for your life. Yesterday, after the battle, which, *vive la France*! we won, we picked you up, lying amid others of the wounded, insensible, and, not knowing from your rags of what nationality you were, we carried you here, so now give an account of yourself. I only trust you are not one of the *sacré* Austrians."

Hébert in a faint voice related all that had befallen him, and only begged one thing, that he might be taken to the Citizen General.

"Citizen General! *Parbleu*, what nonsense; he is deeply engaged; and how do you suppose we can take such a packet of rags as you are to him? We are on the eve of another battle, and he is in the midst of all his preparations for it."

"Just show me his tent so that I may, at least, see his face again," and Hébert's appeals were so pitiful that they at last agreed to his desires.

Having tidied him up as much as possible, two of the soldiers went with him to the entrance of Napoleon's tent; but when he got there, Hébert could not contain himself, and cried, "My general!—my general!" The soldiers remonstrated with him, but his cry had penetrated into the tent, and the voice Hébert knew so well called out, "What is happening? Why all that talk?"

"Oh, it is nothing, Citizen General," replied a sentry; "it is a man of very suspicious appearance who wishes to see you."

"Most likely a fanatical Italian who wishes to kill you," said another.

"What does that matter?" replied Napoleon . "If *I* am not afraid of a dagger, why should you fear for me? Berthier, go and see the man."

Berthier appeared. Hébert called him by his name, spoke of Cairo, Alexandria, the Pyramids, and at the end said: "I am Hébert."

"Hébert? "said the consul, when Berthier returned to him—"Hébert? I remember. Fetch him in."

It is well known what a memory the great general had for names and faces down to the lowest of his soldiers and servants. Therefore, notwithstanding the wretched appearance of his former barber, he recognised him in the twinkling of an eye, and Hébert in a moment saw in his face that he had not forgotten him. Hébert noticed a difference between the general he had lost in Egypt and the great consul whom he found in Italy—a change which in reference to his profession struck him painfully. Napoleon's long hair he so loved to dress had been cut off, which gave his face a sterner appearance than it had before, and Hébert's face fell at the thought he could never plait his pigtail again. However, joy filled his eyes when he heard from a beloved and valued voice the words: "You here, my poor Hébert?"

"I myself. Citizen General. I gave all I had, when I recovered from my illness in Egypt, for a place in the stokehole of a vessel which was returning to Europe."

"And like me you were not taken by the English?"

"No, and on arriving in France, I heard that you had made the inhabitants of St. Cloud jump out of the windows."

"You should have come to me in Paris."

"I did, but you had left for Italy. I followed you here without a penny on me, begging for my bread, and walking all night to escape being taken up, as I was quite determined to join you to show I forgave you for leaving me behind in Egypt."

Bonaparte looked at him steadily, and, putting on a tone of doubtful severity, which generally implied thoughts contrary to his words, said, "Oh, you bear me a grudge! but if I were to be vexed with you for the liberty you have taken? How do you know, sir, that I still want your service—that you have not been replaced?"

"Citizen General, I was in your service in Egypt; I must be the same in Italy."

"Ah, you must! And if I refuse your demand?"
"I would serve you in some way all the same."
"And how, if you please?"
"I would rejoin the ranks and be killed for you."
"Hébert, I was only trying your faithfulness; return here at once. From today I make you my head valet."

Leaving the tent, Hébert was very differently received than on going in. Roustan himself wished to shake hands with him, but the newcomer passed by without looking at the Mameluke, and went to prepare himself for his important duties.

The morning which followed this memorable day was still more remarkable. General Nelas, who had retreated the night before, suddenly reappeared, and with 40,000 men rode to confront the First Consul's 20,000 conscripts. For a moment Napoleon was surprised, but the next sufficed him to develop plans for the bloody battle offered to him. His instructions having been given to his brave officers, Bonaparte became calm, as usual in all the great actions of his life.

Two days after Austria demanded peace, and Hébert clinked glasses with an old friend whom he met on the battlefield. It was one of Lodi's grenadiers of the 32nd, who had just been promoted to the Consular Guard, foundation of the granite column which was afterwards known as *"la Vieille Garde."*

I have no intention in so simple a tale to speak of this glorious period of the consulate, which must be left to a poet. From this source rose the Empire which had its magnificence, but which killed liberty.

You can well understand that Hébert did not belong to those who blamed the actions of the hero. For him he was the essence of divine and human law. Napoleon—Emperor. Hébert was made steward of the Château de Rambouillet, and his old father lodge keeper.

Here Hébert made the acquaintance of a fresh, fair young girl, who pleased him, not for her fortune, but for herself. The Château de Rambouillet became their home, and the emperor gave a dowry to Madame Hébert.

6

It was not generally known, except to those families who had estates in the neighbourhood, that after St. Cloud, the Château de Rambouillet was the emperor's favourite residence.

In the too-short intervals of this long and deadly duel which France waged against the whole of Europe, the Court of Rambouillet was beautiful to see; less grand, but more gay than that of the splendid palace of the Tuileries.

There I have seen nine kings, twenty marshals, and thirty princes, also Eugene, Hortense, Josephine, Marie Louise, and the King of Rome, whose birth had caused the divorce to be forgiven.

Brilliant hunting scenes enlivened the silent forests, but the emperor only took a small part in these pleasures, as war was *his* real pastime. Whilst all these historical persons pursued the stag or the boar, he, driving with Duroc and Berthier, moved at a slow pace along the avenues. There was a little table in his carriage, with many papers on it, and he made notes and memoranda, and dictated his plans for the immortal monuments which he erected all over France, most of them being the outcome of his own brain.

The hunting over, he sprang on one of the Arab horses, which he always rode. He sometimes made a tour of several miles, returning to the *château* by a steep slope, opposite the gate. He always rode down this hill at a gallop. Arriving at the gate, he suddenly stopped his horse, a manoeuvre easy to him, but which often made his followers lose their stirrups when they attempted to imitate it.

I particularly remember a very well-born gentleman, a noble *"rallie de l'ancien régime,"* who never failed to lose his stirrup. He would have been distressed if the "usurper" had perceived his misadventure. He often said in a low voice to his companions, " Bonaparte is a daring breakneck; he will never learn how to ride." These festivities were often interrupted by campaigns, and renewed after victories. Hébert was happy. His wife had been placed at the head of the laundry by the controller of the palace, and to increase their happiness, Madame Hébert presented her husband with two beautiful children, and the eldest was educated by the emperor at the Lycée at Versailles.

Napoleon and Hébert had now arrived at the summit of their good fortune. Alas, fortune soon turned her wheel! The day arrived when all this prosperity began to crumble to its foundation. One army swallowed in the ice of Russia, another destroyed on Spanish soil by Spanish patriots, paved the way to the final annihilation of the Empire. In vain the hero fought with the aid of the brave remnant of his army on French soil; God decided in favour of the Allies.

Napoleon abdicated at Fontainebleau, Hébert had to do so at Rambouillet, and a nobleman demanded from him the keys of the *château*. Hébert wished to follow his master to the Isle of Elba, but 40,000 men asked the same favour, and very few obtained it, and he was not among them. They, perhaps, thought him too faithful.

However, Napoleon had not spoken his last word. The "hundred days" were still to astonish the world, lift up France, and ask her to furnish new armies. At the first news of the emperor's return, Hébert set out for Rambouillet, and the nobleman was obliged to give him back his keys. It was only just.

Alas, this was nothing but a flash of lightning! He who had twice given back their states to Frederick and Francis II, and who had spared Alexander at Austerlitz, was treacherously abandoned by them.

Before leaving France, Napoleon wished to see Malmaison again. There is a great lesson in this simple visit—a great act of repentance. Malmaison! The tomb of Josephine. As General Bonaparte, he found again there the remembrance of his happiness; as the unhappy emperor, the expiation of the greatest of his faults.

Hébert had gone to Paris in hopes of seeing Napoleon and to beg him to let him go with him wherever the "Holy Alliance" fixed the abode of his exile. Vain efforts! Useless devotion! During his absence a simple travelling carriage with two horses stopped before the closed gate of the palace of Rambouillet. This carriage contained four persons: General Becker, Rovigo, Bertrand, and Napoleon. His first words on arriving were: "Hébert—where is Hébert?" Nobody was there to open the gate. Madame Hébert, pale, worn out, hardly able to stand, holding in her feeble hand an enormous bunch of keys, hastened to open the gates and the apartments and to explain her husband's absence.

The emperor stayed that night at Rambouillet, and next day, at the moment of his departure, the poor woman, falling on her knees, covered his hands with tears and kisses. He lifted her, consoled her, and gave orders calmly for the dispatch of some furniture to Rochefort, where he was going. Then, as she still wept, he kissed her on the forehead. She, who was only the wife of a steward, put an empress to shame.

"Tell Hébert that I shall never forget him," were his last words.

When Hébert returned to the palace, he found his wife lying unconscious near a window, from which she had gazed on Napoleon for the last time. From this moment a deadly paleness replaced the fresh colour of her face, a steady growing thinness hollowed her cheeks, and her strength daily diminished.

7

A few retired officers on half pay, some clerks and Lyons merchants, may perhaps still remember a furnished inn, kept by the Héberts in 1817, in Rue de Grenelle-Saint-Honoré, where each paid as much as he could afford, but of ten some did not pay, for the "brigands of the Loire" were very poor for brigands. The business did not go well—indeed, so badly that one day nothing was left to the proprietor but his honour. To add to his misfortune, just at this time he had to carry his dear wife to her last resting-place.

He soon lacked for bread, and would have died of hunger if the Duke of Orleans, since King, had not added his name to the number of workmen who drove the lorries at Neuilly. Hébert earned thirty *sous* a day, but, feeling old age approaching, was more than once inclined to take his life. But one thought took strong hold of his mind; he firmly believed that the emperor would return one day. This last illusion did not last long. Towards the first days of July, 1821, the rumour rapidly spread in Paris that the climate of St. Helena had killed its victim. The fatal news was confirmed, and France had to refuse to receive even the ashes of her hero. Europe was afraid of the very shadow of Napoleon.

All was finished for Hébert; his life seemed to be extinct: his wife and sons had died, and when the news of the emperor's death was confirmed, he put crape on his hat, and determined to wear this mourning for a year, and at the end of it to kill himself.

But the good God did not thus abandon one of His faithful creatures. Heaven owed him compensation—the dearest, the most precious of all: "A remembrance from his emperor."

Napoleon had made a will. (See Napoleon's will). Numerous copies of it soon circulated in France, and beside the names of Muiron, Dugommier, Bertrand, Gourgaud de Larrey, Bessières, and many others, an obscure name was found, a testimony of the gratitude of the "great man." The heart's memory for services performed from the heart.

At the end of one of the codicils of the will, Hébert read these words, through the tears which dimmed his eyes: "20,000 *francs* to Hébert, late steward at Rambouillet, who was my valet in Egypt."

Hébert died some years ago, in comfortable circumstances. Personally, I do not know whom to admire most, the "master," who remembered, or the faithful "servant," who never forgot.

GARDE IMPÉRIALE.

CHAPTER 4

Napoleon as Architect

Napoleon's imagination delighted in designing monuments. Projects of vast construction filled his spare moments more than anything else. He said:

Monuments form the history of nations. Their antiquity is a witness of their civilisation long after its people have vanished, and testifying to their descendants the truth of the victories they might otherwise not believe in.

Napoleon also knew that encouraging fine arts made a reign famous, and preserved in everlasting remembrance the sovereign who encouraged them.

A good monument makes a great name, the louder the noise, the farther it is re-echoed. Institutions and nations fall, but the echo of the noise remains during endless centuries.

The emperor sincerely loved France, and wished his name to be attached to her by indestructible links. All his actions were inspired by instinctive thoughts for her future, and in all his victories his one preoccupation was "the opinion of France," and, like Alexander the Great, who was more proud of having gained the goodwill of the Athenians than of his victory over Darius, the emperor, after the Battle of Austerlitz, said to those round him: "How they will talk of me in Paris!"

During the first days of his Consular power Napoleon called the most skilful architects round him and ordered them to make plans for the restoration of the "*Hôtel des Invalides*." The first thought of the man who owed his rise to power to his military profession, was to embellish the dwellings of his comrades— the witnesses of his glory. "It will be the Elysée of the brave," he said, and for them the most noble of institutions. The Lion of St. Mark, brought from Venice, stood in the middle of the fountain, built in the centre of the esplanade. The four horses from Corinth, the ancient creation of the Greeks, and the trophy of so many victories, had been transported in the course of ages from Greece to Rome, from Rome to Constantinople, from Constantinople to Venice, from there to Paris, and were destined to serve as an *attelage* to the chariot of victory which was placed on the Arc de Triomphe in the Place du Carrousel, consecrated to the Glory of the Grand Army. It is well known that after the Restoration conformable to the Treaty of Paris concluded in 1815 with the foreign Powers, Canova was delegated by Austria to go to Paris to have the horses and also a number of works of art from the Napoleon Museum returned to their own country. The celebrated sculptor, when presented to M. de Talleyrand, Napoleon's ex-Grand Chancellor, was asked: "In what capacity are you sent here?"

"Prince, as an ambassador."

"You make a mistake, you mean as a packer," replied M. de Talleyrand.

After the first campaign in Prussia, Napoleon hardly gave himself time to rest before visiting each room in the Tuileries to examine and judge of the repairs and renovations which had been done during his absence. According to his habit, he criticised everything, and found fault with architects, who, he said laughingly, were "the ruin of empires." Then looking out of one of the windows, he asked M. de Fleurieu, superintendent of the works, why the top of the Arc de Triomphe was covered with canvas. "Sire, it is on account of waiting to see what space is needed for your Majesty's statue, which is to be placed in the car between the two geniuses who guide it."

"What, what does this mean?" exclaimed Napoleon. "I will not have it! "then, turning to M. Fontaine, the architect, he asked: "Was my statue in the design you showed me?"

"No, Sire, it was that of the god Mars."

"Well, why am I to take the place of Mars?"

"Sire, it was not my idea, it was that of M. Denon, my fellow architect."

"Denon acted very wrongly," said Napoleon impatiently. "Flattery, always flattery! And people think they please me by it. The statue must not be erected, it must be taken down; there is no common sense in the idea. Is it for me to have statues of myself erected? Finish off the car and the geniuses, but leave the car empty, do you understand?"

Later on the statue was relegated to the Orange Garden at the Louvre, and was still there in 1830; it was in lead, and remarkable for its resemblance.

In looking over the plans for the Panthéon, he decided to devote the edifice to the purpose for which it was destined. "The High Altar," he said, "will be dedicated to Ste Geneviève, the patron saint of Paris. The coffins which are in the museum of the '*Petits-Augustins*' are to be brought here and arranged according to their dates. They were taken out of temples and should return to one."

At the same time he decided that the Church of St. Denis, which, as he expressed it, "was a vast coffin, filled with the dust of dead sovereigns," and which was being used as a military hospital, should be evacuated, and restored as an Imperial burying-place. He superintended all the changes himself, settled where the small chapel was to be placed, and ordered the names of all the kings to be engraved in brown and black marble and placed against the walls according to their dynasties and ranks. He also made plans for a vault to be constructed for the members of the Imperial Family. But in the midst of the care he gave to works destined to the glory of France and the admiration of strangers, Napoleon showed as keen an interest in connection with improvements of obscure utility which were never likely to be traced to him. Foot-pavements which had been made in Paris in former days had long ceased to exist, owing to the encroachment of shopkeepers on to the road, which made walking very dangerous.

The emperor in one of his *incognito* walks through the streets made a note of this and of the number of accidents arising from it. He at once gave orders to his Minister of the Interior to have the foot-pavements restored as soon as possible, and at the same time to issue an order that every householder should keep the pavement in front of their houses clean. "A workman," he said, "should be able to walk in the streets of Paris without being in danger of slipping on dirty pavements, or in fear each moment of being crushed by the carriages of the rich."

One sees by this that the great statesman, the most powerful monarch in Europe, made an excellent guardian of the city.

While in Spain in 1808, the emperor had given orders that Rambouillet should be prepared for him, as he wished to occupy that beautiful palace on his return. Consequently, it was redecorated and refurnished, as all had been destroyed during the Revolution. Napoleon arrived there in February, and went through the rooms examining every detail. Looking round the bathroom, his eyes showed signs of discontent. "What folly!" he exclaimed to his valet, who was with him; "who could have thought of such a curious idea? Send for the Grand Marshal, Duroc." What had so displeased him was to find the portraits of the ladies of the Imperial Family, including his mother, Josephine, Hortense, and his sisters painted in frescoes, full length on the walls. He kept shrugging his shoulders, saying: "How idiotic!"

When the grand marshal came, he said: "Duroc, send for the painter who has so disfigured these walls, and let him efface these portraits at once. What is his name?"

"Sire, I do not know; he acted under the architect."

"All right, I do not wish to know his name, but all must be effaced. He, whoever he is, cannot have much respect for women to have committed such an indiscretion. He must be a real fool, and must never be employed again."

In all circumstances of his life, the emperor showed great respect for the conventionalities of life. Here is another proof of it. When it was the question of decorating the Place Louis XV with a fountain, the architect presented a plan to him of four *naiads* spouting water from their breasts. This idea displeased him, as he thought it indecent, and he returned the plan to the architect, and said in a cross tone: "Take away these nurses, sir; the *naiads* were virgins."

For a long time past Napoleon had decided on restoring the Palace of Versailles, but the figures of the expenses presented to him by the architect Gaudoin were so enormous, he adjourned it indefinitely. However, in 1809, driving past the palace, after a visit to the School of St. Cyr, he stopped his carriage at the foot of the staircase of the Orangery, called "*les cent marches*," got out, and silently contemplated the imposing mass of buildings which had remained deserted since the Revolution. After a long examination. Napoleon shook his head in the way habitual to him when he had come to a great decision, got into his carriage, and said to the Duc de Vincennes, who was with him, "Decidedly, I must find the six million Gaudoin asks for; I can no longer allow the rats to have possession of the palace and allow it to decay, or else in future ages people will visit Versailles and find it like Babylon, of which there is not a stone left. Versailles is a national possession."

Napoleon then wrote to the architect as follows: "I agree to the sum of six millions being spent on the restoration of the Palace of Versailles, and wish plans to be made out not to exceed that sum, and to include as follows:

1st.—Commodious and comfortable apartments for my family and myself, with private bathrooms.

2nd.—Six sets of apartments for kings, twelve for princes, and twenty-four for Officers of State, and stabling for 200 horses.

3rd.—The side of the palace called '*le Pavilion des Ministres*' to be repaired, and the one on the other side to be pulled down and rebuilt, as its architecture is abominable.

4th.—The *chancellerie*, the servants' apartments, the theatre, and the chapel to be specially restored with care, and decorated with fine and suitable pictures, of which there are many put away in the attics.

5th.—The grand staircase to be entirely reconstructed.

6th.—The buildings of Louis XIII to be demolished; they are devoid of common sense.

7th.—All the great apartments must open one into the other, banning in the left wing and continuing to the right, so as to make them when desired into one long gallery.

8th.—There must also be a fine *salle d'armes*, which will give employment to many in the town, where I wish a manufactory of armour to be established. When all is completed, the palace will be habitable and I shall spend a certain portion of the year there. But before the work begins the architect must sign a contract that he will not exceed the six millions which I am willing to give. If he does, any extra sums he spends will be borne by himself."

It will be seen by this letter, which I have transcribed word for word, how businesslike Napoleon was, and every detail of the plans he passed was carried out to the letter. After the birth of the King of Rome, the emperor desired that a small pavilion should be erected at the end of the terrace looking over the water with a garden round it, where he could breakfast quietly with the empress, and he ordered plans and estimates to be made out. On the architect showing them to him, the estimate came to 500,000 *francs*. "Five hundred thousand *francs*," exclaimed the emperor, "for the pleasure of breakfasting out-of-doors! Ten thousand *francs* I will pay, and no more."

"Sire, it is impossible," replied Gaudoin.

"In that case I prefer to breakfast in my room close to the open window; in this way it will not cost me thirty pence. Five hundred thousand *francs!*" he exclaimed, walking about the *salon*; "now I can well understand how Louis XIV was ruined by his architects. The taste for building is common alike to princes and people. What the people desire is that it should spend itself on national institutions."

Napoleon has been accused of thinking more of celebrity than utility in his many constructions. This is unjust and an error. His principal idea was first to erect buildings combining taste with convenience, and his second to provide work for those classes who had been affected by the war. In 1813, after the victories of Lutzen and Bautzen, his first thought was to call his architects together and consult them on all the work which he wanted to be carried out during his absence in Saxony.

On his return to Paris on November 19th he visited the new galleries of the Louvre. Then he drove to the Halle-au-Blé, where he greatly admired the iron roof erected under the direction of the celebrated Boulanger; he also visited all the markets, followed by an enormous crowd calling out, "*Vive l'Empereur*," offering him in energetic terms their arms to defend him. From there he traversed the Pont Neuf and drove to the Luxembourg, where great works were in hand. At times he complained that some of the works were behindhand, and that all had not been carried out in strict conformity with his plans; but in most cases he was wrong—it was his ideas which had changed.

He returned to the palace by the banks of the Seine, and on his way a small incident occurred which showed how quick his eyes were and that nobody and nothing escaped his notice. In the Champs Elysées among the crowd round his carriage he caught sight of one of his pages. His being there was a breach of discipline, as when in waiting they were forbidden to go out without his permission, or to be dressed as a civilian. The boy had slipped out to see the crowd, never thinking the emperor would notice him, but the surging mass of people carried him close to his master's carriage. He still hoped he had not been noticed, and nearly dropped when, standing behind him at dinner, the emperor called him and, pulling his ear more strongly than usual, said: "Ah, ah, little sir, what were you doing today near the Luxembourg?" The page bent his head and did not even try to justify himself. "Ah, you disguised yourself to play the truant; you know the orders, but you make fun of them, don't you? Perhaps you wanted to spy on me?"

At these words, which the emperor had said in fun, the poor page, who took them seriously, raised his head and looked at the emperor with horror and sadness, which spoke more eloquently than words of the pain such an accusation gave him. Napoleon read his thoughts, and let go of his ear, and, giving him a slight tap on his cheek, which with him was a sign of great good humour, said to him kindly: "There, there, I quite understand; I forgive you, but do not do it again. Think a moment, if all of you went out as soon as my back is turned, who would look after the palace?"

The last order that the emperor gave in January, 1814, a few hours before he started for his admirably planned but fatal campaign, was to give employment of all kinds to the working classes, as he dreaded their being in want.

Tirailleur-Chasseur et Flanqueur-Chasseur.

Officier et Soldat des Marins, grande tenue.

GARDE IMPÉRIALE.

CHAPTER 5

An Egyptian Romance

Napoleon, after his occupation of Egypt, the land of his desire, made Cairo his headquarters, and lost no time in devoting himself to the good of the population: he endowed hospitals, opened free libraries and baths; he released them from many taxes, and bestowed many gifts on the poor. Having done this, he turned his mind to lighter objects, and transformed part of the city into a miniature Paris. Hotels, shops, *cafés*, and a theatre sprang up like magic; the last was placed under the management of an officer of the staff, who undertook to find amateur actors and actresses. Cairo also had its "Tivoli" in the gardens of one of the *pashas*, who placed them at Napoleon's disposal; the gardens were a dream of beauty, redolent with the scent of hundreds of sweet-smelling flowers which grew in great profusion. Winding paths, intersected by rippling rivulets hidden in a forest of palm, orange, and lemon trees, led to little summer-houses, where solitude could be enjoyed, listening to the song of birds of beautiful plumage, and watching their graceful flight to quench their thirst in the stream.

Once a week Napoleon had these gardens opened to the public in the evening, when they were illuminated with thousands of coloured lights. There were fireworks, conjurers, acrobats, dancers, soft music played by hidden musicians, and refreshments laid out in various corners—in fact, nothing was omitted to charm the senses. The variety of costume on these occasions gave further beauty to the scene: the lovely toilets of the ladies, the brilliant uniforms of the officers of the great army, the coloured costumes of the Egyptian population, from those of the *pashas* to the *bernouses* of the Arabs, made a picture impossible to describe.

It was at one of these *fêtes*, which Napoleon always attended, ever wishing to ingratiate himself to the people, that he met Madame

——, a recent bride, who had accompanied her husband. Captain ——, to Egypt. Not many ladies had been allowed to do so; but it was in the middle of his honeymoon that Captain —— had orders to join his regiment, and his general, knowing their devotion to each other, could not resist their united entreaties not to be separated.

Mme. —— was led to Egypt by her conjugal devotion. Whatever annoyance and trouble she suffered was made up to her in love. She regretted nothing; she desired nothing; she was happy! Gifted with the beauty which is neither fair nor dark, neither short nor tall, *madame* was attractive, not in a striking manner, but in a sweet, modest way. Nobody said, "How beautiful she is! "but her graceful figure, her wavy hair, her charming, languid eyes, and her gentle and delicate personality singularly moved the brilliant staff of Napoleon, but the young wife took no notice of her admirers, and the devotion of this couple had remained up till now the envy and edification of all.

Unfortunately, Napoleon was at leisure! Victorious at Arcola, Rivoli, and the Pyramids,—almost a Pharaoh of Egypt, he threw himself at the feet of this lovable dove. Alas, why is it that our human virtues are so fragile, that a breath of wind breaks them, so uncertain that grains of sand swallow them. One man only in the whole army could disturb this calm and happy home, and this man, to whom generally time, opportunity, and will failed, finds that he *has* will, opportunity, and time.

Napoleon saw Mme.—— in the Egyptian "Tivoli" that evening through the prisms of the illuminations and in the midst of the intoxicating music. He saw her and the mischief was done! During the whole evening he kept his profound and expressive look fixed on her. Then, when he saw that little by little he influenced the soul of this lady, he approached her with charming grace, talked a long time, and showed her little attentions, and, so to speak, put his mark on her forehead. She, confused and trembling, was more overcome with pride at this notice than by any other feeling. She felt the honour of this homage, from the rank, the name, the glory of him who laid them at her feet, and from this evening, though in fact still innocent, she was already guilty of disloyalty to her husband.

This feeling would have been without doubt dispelled if Napoleon had applied his obstinacy and his Caesarean ardour to the conquest of her heart. What first he had treated as a passing caprice, became a real and profound passion, and when Mme. ——, after the fascination of the first days, had become sensible again, she opposed this pursuit with innate feelings of her love for and duty to her husband; but the hero at last overcame all obstacles, as opportunities for meeting were not wanting with a man who ruled over all in a military way. General Vernier's wife and the captain's were almost the only French ladies of distinction in Cairo, and their help in the first period of the occupation was useful in establishing intercourse with the Turkish and Christian ladies settled there.

Mme. ―― was thus involved in a political requisition from which she could not withdraw, and gave a pretext for the visits of Napoleon, which from day to day became more dangerous to her. Willing or not, she had also to help to do the honours of the *salon* of the Palace of Esbekieh. Bonaparte did not in the least take advantage of the circumstances. At his age one is generous, one does not hasten love. It was, moreover, at a moment when his soul was troubled on account of Josephine; at the same time the whole strength of his Southern heart sought for outside consolation and satisfaction. Mme. ―― had enough virtue and sense of duty to conquer the first attacks; she was not strong enough to resist the later ones. It is easy to conceive how such an intimacy with such a man awoke passionate exultation and absolute devotion. It seemed to her from that moment that her obscure and modest destiny was to be united to a greater one, and that reflections of Napoleon's luminous glory were to gild her young forehead. Beautiful and transitory illusions!

Nevertheless, a difficulty still existed. The husband was a man of honour. A trick was played on him. He was promoted to the rank of colonel of a cavalry regiment, and received orders to embark immediately for France to convey to the *Directoire* the flags captured from the Mamelukes. He sailed from Alexandria, but his ship was captured by the English near Malta, and he returned to Egypt owing to an exchange of prisoners. His conjugal misfortune was then revealed to him by his comrades, and a divorce became inevitable. It was pronounced before a war commission.

Behold *madame!* Almost Queen of Egypt, and the soldiers called her "Cleopatra." Lodged in Napoleon's palace, always beautifully and richly dressed, she did the honours of her table and was the ornament of her salon. She was good to all, sweet, affable, and witty,—made many and valuable friendships, and distributed favours with grace and discernment. What a golden dream for a woman! She held in her hand, united by a chain of flowers, "the man," whose genius filled the world. She was the heroine of a most beautiful romance in her court, where names such as Monge, Berthollet, Denon, Murat, Eugène Beauharnais proved themselves worthy of fame in the future. She was young and pretty. "To live six months like this and then die," many women would say—not those who clothe their happiness in a chaste garment, but *those* who aspire to brilliant conquests; those who lose their soul in following a meteor.

Napoleon and Mme. —— lived for each other. Beautiful Arab horses were trained for her, and almost every day she followed Napoleon on his most distant excursions, riding by his side, traversing the plains of Gizeh. If he was going to visit the works of the Isle of Radouah, she was with him; if to pay a visit to the old Cheyck-el-Bekri, president of Cairo, she was also there, and drank the coffee of the worthy Mussalman, smoked his pipes, and sipped his perfumed sorbets. She wore the portrait of her hero round her neck. It was a situation of increasing tenderness. When the Syrian expedition was determined on, Mme. —— declared that she would follow the army. She wanted to join the campaign, fight, and perform the duties of an *aide-de-camp*.

This wish was opposed, but to console her for his absence Napoleon promised to write her the most loving letters. Putting aside his military style, as head of the army, he wrote in detail his anxieties, the ravages of the plague, the weariness of the expedition, and his misgivings for the future. These letters still exist. We have had several in our hands, which testify to a tenderness which came from the heart. This love, born in Egypt, and warmed by its sun, lasted in full force till Napoleon decided to leave. The desire for victories elsewhere stifled his love, and his one and sole idea was now to return to France, which he felt was in need of him, and where his great future lay. But to accomplish this he deceived his army, his friends, and his lady love. All was to be sacrificed to his ambition. To the lady he simply said he had to leave on important business for a time, and would soon return. She was a tool in his hand. To his army he also promised a speedy return, and that they would always be in his thoughts.

No one really believed this, and the night preceding Napoleon's departure the poor Ariadne had a presentiment of her approaching abandonment. She went into the palace garden hoping to see him quietly. He was there, but with Generals Monge and Berthier in close conversation. She hid behind the trees, but did not lose sight of him for a moment, watching all his gestures and trying to guess his thoughts, but his countenance was impenetrable. He evidently had seen her, as suddenly she heard him say quite gaily to Berthier, "Good gracious, there is a little lady over there who is watching us," and he then left the garden. Poor Mme. ——, weeping bitterly, retired to her house, and found herself a widow for the second time.

She did not keep her sorrows to herself, and went to General Kléber, whom she knew well, for comfort and advice. She implored him to arrange for her to go to France, and he, being annoyed at being left in Egypt, and tired of the war, or perhaps wishing to cause Napoleon some unpleasantness in exchange for the many worries he had left him to deal with, granted the lovely forsaken woman's request, and arranged that she should sail within a week in the *America*, a French transport, which was to convey Generals Rigel and Lalle to join their master in France.

The misfortunes of our heroine were, however, not ended. The *America* was taken by the English, who landed the passengers at Malta as prisoners, and it was only at the end of four months that Mme. —— was allowed to proceed to Marseilles, where a cruel and bitter disappointment awaited her. Napoleon had rejoined his wife, and in reply to Mme. ——'s letter, telling him of her arrival in France, she received a formal order, sent from Paris, ordering her to fix her residence in Provence, where a house would be provided for her. Later on the first consul was less rigorous. He bought her a beautiful *château* near Paris, and charged one of his trustworthy friends to arrange a suitable marriage for her. A gentleman proprietor was found, whose property was much involved; to make up for this Napoleon gave him a wedding gift of one of the best-paid consulates, so with that, her *château*, her pension, and her new husband, Mme. —— began a new life for the third time.

Napoleon has been accused of having many passions—many of them are inventions, but this is a true one, remembered by many of the old soldiers of Egypt. He did not act as the *roués* of the Regency, or like Tiberias, who had his ladies seized and carried off by force by his Pretorians. Napoleon's devotion was for one woman only at the time, and if he suddenly deserted her, it was not that he was really fickle, but only that such events in his great and powerful mind were just fleeting occasions in his life. He had ever a star before him, a star which guided him in his course of life, and always shook off any fetters that hampered him.

Timballier des chasseurs à cheval (vieille Garde) et Chasseur à cheval (jeune Garde).

GARDE IMPÉRIALE.

CHAPTER 6

The Young Vélite

He was eighteen years of age. His studies were finished. The accounts of the bulletins of the immortal Battle of Austerlitz had fired his imagination. He wished to be a soldier. His father presented him to the general who commanded the department, and he was admitted to the honour of serving in the Imperial Guard as "*vélite*,[1]" On arriving in Paris, he joined a cavalry regiment called "*les Guides*," then the most handsome corps in the army. The spoilt children of the emperor they were called, who knew them all by their names. It was a lucky beginning.

As soon as he was equipped, the young soldier visited a pretty cousin who lived in Paris. She thought him charming in his uniform and wished him success. The praises of the lady cousin flattered and pleased the heart of the cherub so much that he forgot the hour of the roll-call. On returning to the Military School, the brigadier on guard, an old trooper with long reddish moustache and scarred face, ordered him to take off his beautiful uniform and put on his stable coat, cotton trousers, and *sabots*, then took him off to the police court, where he passed the night, lying on straw. Next day the colonel called him, and said:

"Why did you not appear at the roll-call?"

"Sir," replied the poor prisoner in a supplicating voice, "be so kind as to excuse me! I went to see my cousin, and I forgot everything."

"Young man, beware of cousins in Paris. They are more dangerous than the Russian dragoons, for they always hit straight at the heart."

---

1. "*Vélites*" were young men of seventeen or eighteen of good position who were allowed to be attached to regiments on payment to the government of 200 to 500 *francs* yearly. They had to serve in the ranks for a short time, and were eventually incorporated in the Old Guard.

You will leave at once for Versailles, where the instructors will attend to your military education."

After four months' training the *vélite* was considered advanced enough to take part in a great review. It was on the September 15th, 1806. The whole Imperial Guard was assembled at the Carrousel. The emperor rode up, accompanied by a numerous and brilliant staff. Though Napoleon was then only thirty-seven years of age, he was nevertheless one of the oldest of that band of heroes. He passed before the lines at a gallop, then ordered them to form into columns, and, dismounting, walked through the ranks to assure himself of the good state of their weapons, after which he conversed a long time with the surgeon, Larrey, who, after Marshal Bessières, was the man in the regiment the grumblers liked best.

After this the troops manoeuvred with remarkable precision. During the filing by of the ranks the emperor was saluted with vigorous acclamations; but he remained very thoughtful and silent. It was evident that a great project occupied his mind. Next day the infantry was marching towards Prussia, the cavalry and artillery following speedily.

On October 14th Napoleon met the Prussian Army at Jena. This army was still enthusiastic over the remembrance of Frederick the Great, and thought itself invincible. The emperor engaged it in battle and defeated it completely. On that day the children avenged nobly the disasters of their fathers at Rosbach. The cavalry of the Guard was not fortunate enough to assist in this battle, it was still two days behind on its march. At this glorious epoch, victory was so rapid that it was not easy to follow it.

The emperor made his entry into Berlin at the head of his Imperial Guard, and for one month the conquerors enjoyed in the capital of Prussia all the delights of victory.

The young *vélite* had borne well the fatigue of the forced marches. He began to give himself airs. He allowed his sword to sweep the pavement, so that it made a noise, and wore his helmet affectedly over the right ear. Some pretty Berlin ladies, who had taken notice of the fair boy, soon taught him to waltz in the Prussian fashion. The old "*Chasseurs*" had taken to him, because he listened with deference to their long war stories, and also because he was the private secretary of several gentlemen officers, and he never revealed any of their family or love secrets. Soon news came to Berlin that the Russians were coming to the help of King William. Napoleon decided to meet them half-way, and removed his headquarters to Warsaw.

He left this town on December 23rd, and the next day a fierce battle was fought on the way to the Bug. In this fight the *vélite* heard the thunder of cannons for the first time. The field of battle created in him a profound emotion, and when he saw a light artillery battery crossing the plain at full gallop, crushing corpses under the wheels of their munition wagons, his hair stood on end and war appeared to him a most horrible barbarity.

He was full of these painful impressions when Murat rode up in front of the regiment. The prince was dressed in a Polish fur coat, a velvet hat with a diamond clasp, under which his long black curly hair waved round his shoulders. He rode a beautiful Andalusian horse, which he handled with admirable ease. "Gentlemen," he said gaily to the officers, waving his cap like a windmill, "I have come to enable you to give your swords a trial." The regiment immediately advanced, and soon was under the fire of a Russian battery. Shells fell rapidly among their ranks. Many were killed close to the young *vélite*, who thought his last hour had come. Everything helped to fill him with terror. The weather was dull and cloudy. The regiment found itself on the edge of a pine forest, which the imagination of the young man transformed into cypresses. Thousands of crows, birds of ill omen, which the noise of cannons had frightened, flew up from the wood and whirled about in the air, and their dismal cries fell like the sound of a death-knell on the ears of the young soldier. A comrade at his right hand said to him in a low voice, holding out his flask:

"Here, little *vélite*, take a drop of brandy. It is the best remedy."

He had just drunk it when the voice of Murat was heard shouting:

"Trumpeters, sound the charge!"

The raiment dashed forward like lightning on the battery. Two Russian regiments of cavalry rushed to defend it. It became a general *pêle-mêle*, but who could resist the troops led by Murat, who fought like a lion, and gained immortal glory?

The Russians were beaten, and many cannons fell into the hands of the victors.

This terrible, deadly winter campaign continued with varying issues. The emperor was on horseback every morning at daybreak, and rode with his escort to the outposts to head the army on its march. At midday he dismounted; the *chasseurs* lit a good fire and made a shelter for him with straw and branches.

There he received the reports of the marshals, and gave them his orders. The Mameluke Roustam prepared luncheon, and the Mocha coffee was made over the fire in a silver filter. During his halts the emperor had always round him half a dozen *chasseurs* armed with their muskets.

His looks fell on one of them, whose handsome face, though a little pale and still without a moustache, struck him.

"Who placed you in my guard?" he asked him.

"Your Majesty himself" answered the young *vélite*, without hesitation.

"Explain yourself."

"Sire, you published a decree, which permits young men from their eighteenth year to serve in your guard for payment of their board of 300 *francs*. I agreed to these conditions and am now at my post."

"Well, but you are rather small."

"Sire, I do my duty like a *big* man."

"How do you like being a soldier?"

"I think it is sometimes pleasant, but more often very hard. But the chance of seeing your Majesty every day softens the evils and makes me bear privations willingly."

"Have you ever gone through the baptism of fire?"

"Yes, sire, I was at the passage of the Bug."

"Really, it was hot work there. You were frightened, weren't you?"

At this question the young soldier blushed to his ears and looked down in silence.

"You blush; you do not answer," replied Napoleon. "Is it true what I said?"

"Well, yes, sire, I confess I was afraid, but only for a moment."

"Console yourself! There are many others like you." Then, after a moment of silence, . . . "Stop, you are a nice young man. Like others, you have had your experiences. You will lunch with me. Does that please you?"

"Certainly, sire," the *vélite* exclaimed, with great joy at such an honour vouchsafed to him, and he laid down his gun.

Roustam served him with some slices of ham on a silver plate, with all the ceremony he would have shown to a great officer of the Empire. The *vélite* enjoyed it as every young man would, and still more so after several days of small rations, and when the Mameluke poured the Chambertin into a silver-gilt cup. Napoleon said smilingly:

"Ah, ah, my boy, you will be glad to drink your wine out of a goblet, as one cannot judge how much you drink. Is it filled up to the brim?"

"Yes, sire, up to the brim, but with a full glass I shall drink your Majesty's health better."

During the time of this improvised luncheon Napoleon conversed constantly with his young guest, who replied with respect and brightness. After the coffee the emperor asked his name.

"Sire, my name is Laurain."

"Very well. Monsieur Laurain, we have made acquaintance. Conduct yourself well! I shall see to your promotion when the time comes."

The *vélite* expressed his thanks, bowed, took up his gun, and went away to attend to his duties.

The campaign ended with the Battle of Friedland and the glorious Treaty of Tilsit. The Guards returned to Paris. Napoleon, hunting in the environs of Trianon, wished to see the *vélites*, so he rode into Versailles where they were garrisoned. They formed in line before him, and he said to Commander Francq: "Order Vélite Laurain who lunched with me in Prussia to come forward."

"Sire," replied the commander, "your Majesty made him an officer of the Hussars, who are at present in Spain."

"Why have they sent him there; he is still so young."

"Sire, he slew with his own hand two big Russian grenadiers in view of the whole regiment."

"That's different. He deserved it. I shall meet him somewhere else."

Alas, the unfortunate young man never saw his emperor again. He had the misfortune to fall alive into the hands of Spanish bandits, who horribly tortured and killed him.

He bore all with heroic courage, and, before breathing his last, uttered one word—the name of his cousin.

Officier de Chasseurs à pied, grande tenue; Fusilier-Chasseur, tenue de route, et Conscrit, grande tenue.

GARDE IMPÉRIALE.

Officier de voltigeurs et Garde national, grande tenue.

GARDE IMPÉRIALE.

Chapter 7

After Jena

After the Battle of Jena, the first order that Napoleon gave to one of his *aides-de-camp*, on entering Berlin on October 27th, 1806, was to go immediately to the post office and seize all the letters. Among them was one addressed to the King of Prussia. On being opened, it was found to have been written and signed by Prince Hatzfeld, who had been left at Berlin as Napoleon's representative during the provisionary government in Prussia. In this letter he gave his sovereign a detailed account of all that had happened in the capital after his departure, and added remarks by no means flattering to Napoleon, and gave an exact description of the strength of troops and munitions and of the number of our artillery guns in the city.

As a prince had written this letter, it was at once handed to the emperor. Napoleon read it carefully several times, and at intervals exclaimed, " But this is abominable! Oh, how base and treacherous! No one can blame me if I have him shot, after trial by court martial."

Biting his lips, he put the letter in his pocket and immediately gave orders for the arrest of the prince. But luckily for the accused Napoleon forgot to send the only proof of his guilt—the letter to the King of Prussia.

The emperor, left alone with Berthier, then ordered him to sit down and write the order for the court-martial. The general protested. Napoleon lost patience and struck the bureau with both clenched fists so violently that everything fell off. Berthier rose quietly and left the room. The emperor, ashamed of his passionate outburst, could not speak, but stood motionless with folded arms, following Berthier with his eyes.

When he was a bit calmer he called Rapp, his *aide-de-camp*, from the ante-room.

"Rapp," said he, "sit down here and write."

The *aide-de-camp* hesitated.

"Come, come! make haste if you can!" cried Napoleon, stamping his foot. Then walking backwards and forwards, dictated the following words:

"On receipt of this, our cousin Marshal Davoust will immediately appoint a military commission, consisting of himself as president and seven colonels of his corps, to judge Prince Hatzfeld as convicted (underline 'convicted,' he interrupted) of treason and espionage. Judgment must be given and the sentence carried out (underline 'carried out,' said the emperor, emphasising the words) today, before six o'clock. The troops of Marshal Davoust's *'corps d'armée'* are to be present when sentence is given, also when it is carried out."

Napoleon, taking the pen from Rapp's hand, read what he had just dictated in a low voice, and signed the paper, saying, "That's done."

Then changing his tone and addressing Rapp with the familiar "*tu*," he said, "You, at least, obey me; you have faith in your emperor, you are his friend, and will not play him false as others do." Then taking Prince Hatzfeld's letter from his pocket, said, "Come! dispatch this order quickly and take this with it."

Rapp,[1] however, did nothing of the sort, although fearing the more in consequence for himself and the prince. Moreover, instead of taking the previous order of arrest to Davoust he had left it in the palace. Now saying "Come what will of it," he put both letters in his pocket.

Later in the day rumours of the arrest had reached Princess Hatzfeld. Wild with grief, she hastened to the palace, and was imploring the Grand Marshal, Duroc, to intercede in her husband's behalf when suddenly the cry "Present arms!" followed by the beating of drums, announced Napoleon's return to the palace. The grand marshal hurriedly left the princess and went to meet the emperor, who had already reached the top of the staircase.

Napoleon, surprised, said, "Well! has anything fresh happened?"

"Yes, Sire," Duroc replied.

"Follow me then," said the emperor, hurrying on; "we will see to it."

He was just entering the first *salon* when a woman burst in from one of the ante-chambers and threw herself, weeping, at his feet. "Justice, Sire, justice!" cried the poor princess.

---

1. Rapp: the Last Victor by Jean Rapp is also published by Leonaur.

Count Bertrand

Napoleon gently raised her, gave orders that no one should be admitted, and entered his" private room, followed by Rapp, who was supporting the princess. "Poor woman! poor woman," the emperor murmured several times, for he thought the orders of the morning had been carried out. After motioning her to an armchair near the fireplace, he whispered to Rapp, "Send immediately to Davoust to postpone judgment."

The *aide-de-camp*, for answer, and with eyes cast down, handed a paper to Napoleon.

"What is this?" and tearing open the envelope the emperor saw the prince's letter which he had given to Rapp some hours before. With a look which seemed to pardon his disobedience, he said in a low voice, "I forgive you." Then turning to the princess, "Now, *Madame*, speak, I am at liberty to hear you."

The poor lady complained bitterly that her husband had been unjustly accused, for she was certain he had never acted as a spy or traitor.

Napoleon, seated in front of her, listened patiently with legs crossed and elbows resting on the arms of his large chair gazing at his thumbs, which he was turning one over the other the whole time she was speaking.

When she had finished he rose, saying benignly, "Well, *Madame*, you must know that your husband has brought himself into a grave position, and according to our law has incurred the penalty of death. Here," he said, handing her the fatal letter, "take it, read it."

The poor woman gazed in terror at the accusing evidence, and, as she read, horror spread over her face, and in her stupefaction she could only murmur these words: "Oh, my God, sire, it is indeed his writing!" She then gazed at Napoleon fixedly, and fell on the floor, and with streaming eyes held out her arms to him. "Ah, sire, pardon, for my children's sake, and for my own, for I am expecting another child," she said in accents of despair.

"*Madame*," said Napoleon, coming close to her, "without this accusing letter there would be no proof against your husband."

"Alas, sire, that is a truth I cannot deny!"

"Therefore," he continued, "I see no other way but to burn it."

The princess still held the letter in her trembling hands, not understanding what Napoleon meant. She did not know what to say or what to do, when Napoleon, seeing her indecision.

"Act, act, *Madame*, just as you would do if you were alone." And, seeing her still hesitating, added: "Well, let me help you," and, taking her by the arm, led her to the fireplace, and with his other hand took the letter out of her hand and threw it into the fire, saying, "Now, Madame, your: husband is pardoned. I have no longer any proof." Then, without waiting for her thanks, he called Davout and bade him conduct her back to her home.

The next day in his daily letter to Josephine,[2] he wrote as follows:—

My dearest one,

I have received your letter, in which you reproach me for having a poor opinion of women. It is true that beyond all things I hate intriguing women, who lead their husbands by the nose. I only care for good and tender-hearted women like you. If they spoil me, it is not my fault. However, you will be pleased to hear that I have today been very kind to a poor lady, who proved to me her great love for her husband, whose death sentence I reprieved. If I had seen her some hours later it would have been too late. Her devotion to her husband, which I saw was genuine, saved his life, and now she is with him happy and tranquil. From this you see I love women who are sweet and faithful; why? Because they resemble you.

Adieu,
  Ever thine,
    Napoleon.

---

2. Napoleon's Letters to Josephine by Henry Foljambe Hall is also published by Leonaur.

Chevau-Légers lanciers (deuxième régiment), et Tartares lithuaniens, attachés comme éclaireurs au régiment de chevau-légers lanciers.

GARDE IMPÉRIALE.

Le Prince J. Poniatowski, commandant en chef les troupes polonaises.

GARDE IMPÉRIALE.

CHAPTER 8

A Halt During the Campaign in 1815

In this short campaign Napoleon's sublime inspirations did not seem to guide him as they did in Italy.

After the defeat of one *corps d'armée* he felt his army needed repose, and hoped to be able to arrange an armistice with Prince Schwartzenberg, who, when advancing on Paris, had been defeated and obliged to retreat. Napoleon knew that Soissons was in a good state of defence with a strong garrison, and he had a plan of attacking Blücher in the rear, and of drawing him into a trap.

Unfortunately, this plan failed through the treachery of General Moreau, who, while Napoleon was preparing to attack Blücher, surrendered Soissons to General Bulow, and this ensured the free passage of the Allies to the Aisne. On hearing this bad news. Napoleon exclaimed: "The name of Moreau will ever be fatal to me!" His troops, owing to this disaster, were deprived of the repose Napoleon had planned for them, and the next morning they were on the march to fight Blücher, but, before leaving the village where they had bivouacked. Napoleon sent for the mayor, and gave him a sum of money for the poor, and for the reparation of the church and buildings destroyed by the Prussians. He also interviewed the doctor, and, recognising in him one who was with him in Egypt, decorated him, and bade him give all his care to any sick or wounded of the army that might be sent there.

Ill-fortune seemed now to follow Napoleon's footsteps; serious dispatches brought him news that Blücher was advancing on both sides of the Marne at the head of 80,000 Prussians towards Meaux, while Schwartzenberg, being informed of this move of the Prussian generals, cut short all armistice negotiations, and marched with a large force to take the offensive at Bar-sur-Seine. Napoleon, whose genius took in rapidly all the enemy's operations, but who could not be himself everywhere at once, resolved to proceed in person against Blucher with the greater part of his army, and sent the other corps to intercept Prince Schwartzenberg; but the loss of a huge convoy of guns, powder, bombs, and ammunition of all kinds, which were captured by the enemy, delayed his march, and a halt had again to be made at the small village of Herbisse, where Napoleon determined to spend the night. The Presbytery had been selected in advance by Berthier, as the emperor's headquarters.

On seeing the emperor and his suite approach, the *curé* was beside himself with joy and surprise, mingled with nervousness, but Napoleon soon put him at his ease, for dismounting from his horse and entering the house, he said, "*Bonjour*, my dear *curé*, we are only come to beg your hospitality for one night. We will make ourselves very small and not give you any trouble." He then established himself in the only downstairs room, which served as a kitchen and dining-room. It was small and very damp, and the Prince de Wagram, asking the emperor what he would do in such mean quarters, Napoleon replied, laughingly: "I shall certainly feel more comfortable than those two gentlemen," pointing to myself and another officer who had just entered covered with mud, having fallen into a dirty ditch, hidden by some bushes, which gave us a lamentable appearance.

The emperor then leant over a table covered with maps and dispatches, studying them with as much calm and attention as if he had been at the Tuileries. The officers made arrangements for sleeping in a small cottage near the Presbytery. The provision canteen shortly arrived, and, there only being one table in the room, another was improvised by putting some shutters on planks, and those who could not sit ate standing.

The emperor sat with the *curé* on one side and the Marshal Lefèvre on the other, and all did honour to the simple repast, which consisted of cold beef, an excellent omelette, and some apples. These last were the *cure's* contribution, besides some wine of the country. The naive good nature of the host made the meal one of the gayest. The emperor wanted to hear every detail of the poor parish and its inhabitants, which the *curé* gave him. He was lost in astonishment at the knowledge Napoleon had of the topographical position of Herbisse and its environs, which culminated when the major-general pulled out of his pocket a plan on which were marked the smallest details of the neighbourhood. There was an amusing scene between the *curé* and Marshal Lefèvre, as the latter suddenly began quoting Latin bearing greatly on religious subjects, which much surprised the *curé*, who at last said: "Sir, you should have been in the Church instead of the army."

Lefèvre then explained that he had been destined to be a priest, but, after having studied for some time for this vocation, his inclinations changed and he took to the sword instead.

"*Monseigneur*," the *curé* said, "what a pity, with all your learning. I feel sure you would have become at least a cardinal one day."

"How at least?" replied Lefèvre. "You mean that I might have been Pope?"

"And why not?" said one of the *aides-de-camp*, "and if our host had been a sergeant in '89, he might have been a marshal like you."

"Or dead," added the Duc de Dantzic, "and far better for him, for he would not see the enemy thirty *lieues* from Paris."

"Oh, *monseigneur*," said the *curé*, reverently making the sign of the cross, "with God's help, and that of the emperor, we shall conquer."

"Yes, yes," murmured the duke, "but we must be ready to meet whatever fate awaits us." And hastily changed the conversation.

But when supper ended and all sought repose, the emperor did not undress, but simply lay down on the *curé's* bed, giving orders to be called up if anything occurred. The night passed quietly, and at 4 a.m. the emperor was up and went round to his officers to wake them.

"Wake up!—wake up, sirs!" he said, giving them a gentle push. "You are all very lazy; quick, quick—on horseback, all of you!"

And in a few moments we were all on the move, but not without Napoleon bidding farewell to the hospitable *curé* and slipping into his hand a one-thousand *franc* note.

Alas, there were not many peaceful halts to be chronicled after this!

Sapeur du génie, grande tenue et tenue de travaux.
GARDE IMPÉRIALE.

Aide-de-camp attaché à l'État-major général, et Gendarme d'ordonnance.
GARDE IMPÉRIALE.

CHAPTER 9

At Erfurt

In 1808, Napoleon and Alexander had arranged to meet at Erfurt, a small town in Saxony, and a dependency of the Grand Duchy of Frankfort. The meeting took place on September 27th. All the small sovereigns of Germany, grand dukes and princesses, had also assembled there. Others arrived from the banks of the Danube, the Rhine, and the Baltic. They came to pay homage and renew their protestations of devotion to the hero crowned by victory, protector of the Confederation of the Rhine, distributor of thrones, and maker of kings.

The Emperor of Austria and the King of Prussia were alone absent. Napoleon had vanquished and pardoned them, and returned their kingdoms to them, but he had not admitted them into his confidence with regard to future projects, as he had done with Alexander. M. de Vincent, the Ambassador of Austria, and the young Prince William of Prussia were there, to watch events and to meditate on the value and sanctity of a royal alliance. No notice was taken of them by their former courtiers, who all gathered round Napoleon and Alexander. The kings and princes were lodged in various quarters of the town, many over the shops of the rich shoemakers, whose industry enriched Erfurt by supplying other countries with their goods. Napoleon and Alexander were separately and more sumptuously housed.

Talma had arrived with Mlle. Duchesnois, and the chief actors of the *Théâtre Français*. Napoleon had promised him a *"parterre de rois."* Talma, king of theatres, therefore comes like Napoleon, to take possession of a new domain, and what a theatre was that of Erfurt! A palace—a palace worthy of Augustus— of Sémiramis. It could rival in elegance that of Limoges and many others, but what mattered the theatre, what mattered the play, what mattered the actors? The audience alone absorbed the attention. Those who composed it were the sole, the true actors of the play.

On the night of the first performance the boxes filled rapidly, as all knew that Napoleon would be as exact in arriving at the hour fixed as if attending a military review. Princesses, ladies-in-waiting, young and beautiful women, richly dressed and resplendent in jewels, formed a brilliant and sparkling girdle round the theatre. Among them were the Princess Stephanie de Beauharnais and Catherine of Würtemberg, the first married to the Grand Duke of Baden, and the latter to Jérôme Bonaparte, and therefore Queen of Westphalia. There were many princesses of Germany who had not disdained to marry Frenchmen, although they were not princes. Eugène de Beauharnais, that brave, noble young man, had just married Princess Amelia, eldest daughter of the King of Bavaria; Berthier, who was neither young nor handsome, married later on Princess Elizabeth, niece of the same king. France was then *the great Nation*. Since her sun has set, these marriages have ceased. In a corner of one box Mlle. Bourgeois, the actress, was seen. She may have thought that "Iphigenia," lovely woman as she was, would not be out of place in this new "Aulide." The prefect of the palace, however, informed her that, although she might be queen of the stage as much as she liked, off it this *rôle* was absolutely forbidden her, and she had to retire.

As we look round the theatre again, we see all the places filled up, with the exception of one box in the centre, reserved for the two emperors. There is no orchestra; its place is taken up with seats occupied by the Kings of Saxony, Würtemberg, Westphalia, Prince William of Prussia, and the Austrian Ambassador. The King of Westphalia saluted the Queen in her box, and all the kings saluted M. de Talleyrand and Berthier, who were in a corner one. It was sad to see the King of Saxony, Frederick Augustus, that honest man, bow to him who made fools of all kings, M. de Talleyrand, and whose mysterious smile seemed to say: "Kings are placed on earth to amuse us."

Following the King of Saxony was Maximilian Joseph, King of Bavaria, known formerly in France as Prince de Max, colonel of the old Regiment of Alsace, when colonels worked embroidery and made nets. By the obsequious salutation which this new king made to M. de Talleyrand, it was evident that he had not laid aside his habits of a courtier nor would he recognise the humility of his position. Please note that to Prince Max of the Alsace Regiment we owe the receipt for "*bavaroise au lait*," and he was more proud of this than of anything. The King of Würtemberg was the last to arrive, almost bent double from the weight of his fat body. Whether it was his strong and powerful countenance which commanded respect is not known, but it was noticed that M. de Talleyrand did not smile so ironically as he had done before.

Among other royalties were the Grand Dukes of Baden, Weimar, Hesse, Darmstadt and Wurtzberg, Constantine, brother of the Emperor Alexander, the Dukes of Nassau and of Holstein Oldenburg, two Dukes of Mecklenburg, three Dukes of Saxony, and Princes of Anhalt, Hohenzollern, and Reuss, etc. Councillors, ministers, and chamberlains in magnificent uniforms, and orders and decorative scarves of every colour, were assembled ready to receive the king of kings; all eager to have a smile or a single word addressed to them. But no time was given to this. To the sound of trumpets and drums, the two emperors entered, and, bowing to all quickly, went to their box. No one had hardly time to rise from their seats to salute them before the curtain rose and the play began. Such was the etiquette followed at Erfurt, an etiquette which froze everything; the theatre was cold, the spectators were cold, the actors were cold; no enthusiasm and no illusions. But for some wonderful acting by Talma and Duchesnois, which the illustrious spectators much admired, they were certainly royally bored.

Let us remove our eyes from the royal spectacle and carry them to the hall of the theatre. Here the Crosses of the Legion of Honour outsparkled all the decorations, like stars among their satellites, on the breasts of many brave French officers, among whom the Duc de Vincent and the Duc de Montebello stood out prominently. One spectator, seated in a corner of the theatre, and who wore no decoration, paid the greatest attention to Racine's beautiful verses. He was quite solitary amid this gilded crowd, and evidently deeply felt and appreciated each word to which he listened.

The play ended, the emperors rose together, and retired with the same solemnity as on their entrance. Napoleon alone saluted with an affectionate smile the silent spectator we have referred to. He saluted him, not because he was the minister or councillor of the Grand Duke of Weimar, but because he was the man of genius, Goethe. The kings disappeared, the princes followed; the boxes were cleared, and all appeared to have been a dream. Thus ended the first theatrical performance at Erfurt. It was followed by four others, when Cinna, Andromaque, Britannicus, and Zaïre were acted.

The same royalties were present at each performance, the same

Conférences D'Erfurt Napoleon receiving De Vincent, Austrian Minister

etiquette was followed, and the same dullness prevailed. The two emperors left Erfurt on October 14th.

A library in the town at that date announced the production of a book under the title of *Erfurt in its Greatest Splendour, illustrated with the Portraits of all the Sovereigns*.

We do not know if the work was ever published, but, with the exception of Napoleon, whose life is so wonderful, splendid, and powerful, all the other celebrities' portraits who were at Erfurt have been singularly forgotten.

Voltigeur et Flanqueur-Grenadier.
GARDE IMPÉRIALE.

Officier d'achevaux de l'Empereur
GARDE IMPÉRIALE.

CHAPTER 10

New Year's Day in the Palace of Saint Cloud

PART 1

The Empress Josephine in her heart possessed ail the treasures of maternal tenderness. These feelings were very deep, and showed themselves in her love for children. She delighted in entertaining them, having them round her, and in giving them presents. Not a week passed without her buying magnificent toys, and distributing them herself at the parties she gave them. The *boudoir* of the empress at St. Cloud often resembled a toy shop in the Arcades. But it was especially at the New Year this charming bazaar was laid out. On entering the room, which served as an ante-chamber to the others, one might have been in one of the galleries of Alfonso Giroux. In it were heaped up "toys, jewellery, china, and boxes of *bonbons.*" There were dolls bigger than the little girls to whom they were to be given; drums and trumpets, cavalry and foot regiments of leaden soldiers, forts, swords, etc., were to be the joy of the boys.

For January 1st, 1805, Josephine had issued invitations to a select number of her friends, with their children, for a party to be given by her at St. Cloud. From early morning on that day the empress saw to the unpacking of the presents, which were all sent from Paris. She herself arranged the gifts, writing the name of each child on the present destined for it. Jewellery, rich materials, silver articles, etc., for the eldest girls; magnificently dressed dolls, dinner sets, tea sets, etc., for the smaller ones; watches, writing-cases, etc., for the elder boys; every kind of musical instrument, soldiers, suits of armour, balls, puzzles, etc., for the younger ones.

By three o'clock on the happy day all the guests had arrived and were received by the Empress in the ante-chamber, from which she led them into the large hall, where all the gifts were laid out. Shrieks of delight broke out from all, and eager eyes gazed on the coveted gifts, and when each boy and girl received theirs, the empress gave them a sweet kiss, which greatly added to the value of the gift.

Great as was the babel before, it then became ten times greater, and at last the empress put her fingers to her ears and retired to her private room, some little way off, with the mothers, so as to let the children be free to amuse themselves as they liked. All went smoothly at first, but ere long disagreements began to arise on all sides. The little boys had decided unanimously to play at war, and tried to force the little girls to join them. They opposed the idea in a body, and protested loudly against it, when young Achille Zaluski, son of a Polish general, naturalised French (for whom Napoleon had the greatest respect), who had made himself leader of the troop, decided that those little girls who had shown themselves the most rebellious were to be provisionally shut up in the "*citadelle*," and to remain there until they consented to obey the new order of conscription, by coming to place themselves under the flag.

Now, the "*citadelle*" was nothing less than Josephine's delightful *boudoir*, close to the hall, lighted by small windows with curtains of green silk, embroidered with silver bees. For a moment it was a question of improvising a council of war, of judging and even shooting little Emma, who appeared to be at the head of the opposition party, when, fortunately for her, Mme. de Larochefoucault, one of the empress's ladies, hearing the noise, came to interpose with her authority, and threatened M. Achille with only dry bread for supper if he did not let the little girls play together as they liked best, but fearing that they might still be worried, she made the boys go into the "*citadelle*" to play by themselves. Once separated, there were no more quarrels, but the noise was greater than ever, only replaced by hearty laughter. Josephine was delighted. Meanwhile, Napoleon had arrived at St. Cloud to do some work quietly, and his private room was exactly above the *boudoir*. He went to his wife's apartments and asked her in a half-gay, half-serious tone the cause of the noise. Josephine told him.

"You ought," he replied, "to distribute the presents when I am *not* there. I shall go myself and ask the little guests to make less noise, and if they continue . . ."

"Let the poor children enjoy themselves," said Josephine. "The boys are playing at war; the little girls are dancing. You will frighten them if they see you; I will send somebody to keep them quiet."

"Ah, they are playing at war," repeated Napoleon, smiling; "that will be interesting; I should like to see how they set about it." And going on tiptoe, rubbing his hands, the emperor went to the door of the hall. He listened for a moment, and only distinguished these words: "Forward! Fire! I have killed him! It is not true! Yes, just see! . . . Dead! . . ."

Amid the loud cries and shouts of echoing voices, the emperor opened the door and showed himself.

"Well, what is this?" he said, in a severe tone. "What is all this noise about?"

At these words the little troop looked up, and all remained motionless from surprise and fear. The emperor gazed at this gathering of small ones with delight. Each child was more charming than the other, and he could not help smiling at the grotesque manner in which they were dressed up. One had made a three-cornered hat out of paper, and had fastened on it a large macaroon as a cockade; another had hung his coat over his shoulder to represent the dolman of a hussar. Little Adolphe, a good-looking boy, had painted himself a moustache with China ink, and with the fur cape of a little girl had made a belt into which he stuck a paper knife of mother-of-pearl as a dagger. His sleeves were turned back to the elbow, and he held a pistol in each hand. Under this disguise little Adolphe looked so full of mischief that Napoleon sat down in order to watch him more leisurely. He then made him a sign to approach and took him on his knees.

"What's your name, *monsieur?*" he asked, trying to be serious,

"My name is Adolphe?"

"I bet it was you who shouted the loudest a little while ago!"

"Gracious me! No, it was Achille, who did not want me to be the general, and wanted to be one himself."

"That is not fair; each should have his turn. And where is this Monsieur Achille?"

"Down there; he who has the armour on." And Adolphe, turning round, pointed with his finger to a boy a little bigger than himself who had made a breastplate out of a music-book cover, on which he had fastened a star of sugar candy.

"Ah, ah," continued Napoleon, "I must speak to this Monsieur Achille, who wants to be master here," and, gently patting Adolphe's cheek, the emperor sent him away and called up Achille. The latter approached, running and jumping, and with a swift bound placed himself astride the emperor's knees, who said: "What is your father's name. Monsieur Achille?"

"General Zaluski."

At this name Napoleon's expression brightened, his eyes sparkled, he drew the child close to him, and, looking at him with tenderness, said, "Zaluski, you say; he is one of my great friends, and a brave one! And what will you be one day?"

"I—I shall be what papa is. I shall wear two large gold epaulets and have a sharp sword."

"Dear me, what will you do with it?"

"I shall kill all our enemies."

"Really, but I hope that henceforward we shall not have any more."

"And then," added the child, "I shall wear round my neck a beautiful red ribbon like papa, with a fine large real star of honour, not like this," and Achille took the sugar-candy star which he wore, and broke it with his teeth.

"Oh, that's another matter," replied the emperor. "You do quick business. How old are you now?"

"I shall be twelve on mamma's birthday."

"Well, perhaps in twenty years' time."

"But I wish for all this much sooner. Papa told me that I shall be an officer at the age of eighteen."

"Your father judges from himself. Of course that depends on yourself. In the meantime, in case you should break your present sword, here is forty *francs* to buy another; now go and play with your friends, and do not make quite so much noise." Then, turning to all the children, he said: "*Adieu*, my little friends, amuse yourselves well, but do not have any real fights; I forbid it."

Napoleon's orders were not carried out to the letter, as Adolphe, jealous at seeing Achille so favoured, tried to get up a quarrel with him, which might have become serious if the doors had not been thrown open and "Supper is ready" announced in a loud voice by a servant in green livery. All quarrels were at once ended, and the children were only too delighted to be formed in rows according to their height, and marched into the dining-saloon, where the empress awaited them, and saw them seated at a large table, which groaned beneath the luxuries with which it was covered, and of which the children soon showed their appreciation. The repast over, all returned laden to their homes in joy and delight.

Part 2

Nine years had passed. It was at the beginning of 1814 when Europe, which till then had been subservient to Napoleon's rule, allied itself against him. After many victories. Napoleon, strong, in his belief of his good fortune, encamped on March 6th at Craone, we might almost say in the middle of Russian bivouacs which were concentrated on all the surrounding points. Here, during the night, he reconnoitred all the enemy's positions, and at daybreak his whole army was ready for the battle, and opened fire with the cry of "*Vive l'Empereur.*" A height was taken and retaken, the possession of which would determine the success of the day, and the battle raged furiously. Four o'clock came and nothing was yet decided. Napoleon cast his eye on his Old Guard, who remained behind him, like himself immovable, but impatient. He had only one word to say: "Advance," and this word he was on the point of saying when suddenly a young officer arrived at a gallop, pulled up his horse, and, holding up his hand, proudly cried: "My emperor, my emperor, we are masters of the height!"

"At last," cried the emperor; "all honour to our brave men," and was just starting off on his horse to view the captured height when, looking at the officer to say a kind word to him, he saw his pallid face and bloody uniform, and that he seemed hardly able to keep his seat on his horse. The emperor bade him dismount, saying, "Are you badly injured? Who is your general?"

"Sire," he said, with a faltering voice, "my general is killed, and I, I . . ." he could say no more, and lay on the ground sobbing.

"Take the greatest care of him," Napoleon said, in a tender voice. "But just wait one moment," and, detaching his cross of honour, he laid it on the breast of the young officer, whose strength was fast failing. He made a last effort, seized the emperor's hand, and kissed it, and in a whisper, said: "Sire, I die happy; some years ago at St. Cloud, when I was twelve years old, I prayed to be worthy one day to wear this cross—I, Achille Zaluski.—Tell my father I have won it—as to my poor sister . . ." These were his last words; all was over.

Napoleon sobbed, and murmured, "Yes, yes, brave boy, I remember it all," and he hid his face for a few moments, then gave orders that he should be buried with all honours, and with his staff proceeded to his tour of inspection.

The next day the funeral took place in accordance with Napoleon's directions.

Two days afterwards he sent for General Zaluski. "General," he said, in a grave voice, "your son has fallen bravely on a Field of Honour."

"Yes, sire."

"He has a sister, has he not?"

"Yes, sire, she had only him and me."

"And me also," Napoleon said quickly. "You are leaving me out. I will at once place her in my Imperial Institution at Ecouen, and I will settle her marriage portion when the time arrives. I decorated your son before he died. I make you this morning Chevalier of the Legion of Honour."

"Thanks, thanks, sire! but oh," bursting into tears, "my poor son! Nothing can replace him."

Napoleon went up to him, and, putting his arms round him, said in a broken voice, "Pity your emperor, and embrace him, for he also is very miserable and suffers in seeing others suffer."

Mlle. Zaluski went to the Institution, where she was well cared for; but as to her marriage portion. Napoleon could, alas! not give it, as he was mourning for a son in his exile at St. Helena. The memory of Achille never left his sister. Lately, in talking to her, the eyes of the poor girl were bathed in tears, and silently she showed me, hanging over the fireplace in a deal frame, a child's wreath of laurel and everlastings, and near it a small sword and the Cross of the Legion of Honour; the wreath was one Achille had been given at the Lycée Imperial, the sword was one of the gifts given him at St. Cloud by the empress, and the cross was the one which Napoleon had laid on his breast as he breathed his last sigh.

Vivandière, Soldat du train des équipages et Ouvrier d'administration.

GARDE IMPÉRIALE.

E. Bellangé 1860

LA RETRAITE DE RUSSIE

GENERAL BERTHIER

CHAPTER 11

The Tomorrows

One of the greatest and most extraordinary faculties of Napoleon was the power of concentrating all his attention to one given point. At Marengo, Austerlitz, Jena, Eylau, Friedland, Wagram, etc., he had only one idea, "Victory." Victory attained, his thoughts at once reverted to all other interests which he had laid aside for the one pressing object. He lost the vivacious manner which he had during the combats, and his countenance again assumed its usual gravity, and his thoughts became once more impenetrable. On the eve of a battle, before taking a moment's rest, he retired to his tent and spent some time with his major-general. "Well, Berthier," he said, in a hurried manner, before the Battle of Wagram, "tomorrow will be our great day. We have the game in our hands. Hurry up the orders! We must fire the guns without waiting for the explosion of their bombs. Quick"—he said to his secretary—"write the orders, which I will dictate to you," and then, sitting at the corner of a table covered with maps, transmitted to paper the manifold orders for all the commanders of the Great Army, as rapidly as pen could write.

Next day during the battle the emperor's eagle eye seemed to be everywhere at the same moment, giving numerous orders, watching them being carried out, and never leaving the battlefield till the certain results of the day were known. In the evening he would find hundreds of dispatches piled up in his tent, all demanding his close attention. He always dictated those sublime bulletins which informed France that she might inscribe another victory in her glorious annals. With the help of the Duc de Bassano he transmitted orders to certain of his ministers in Paris, of special work he wished them to undertake. Amid all this, he never lost sight of what was going on around him, and never avowed a victory till really complete.

The next morning at daybreak he visited the battlefield to make sure himself that all the wounded had been moved into the temporary hospitals, which he afterwards visited, going all through the wards, comforting and consoling each man, bestowing rewards on those who deserved them, and in the case of those who could not live he soothed their last moments by promising to look after their families, so that they should never suffer from want. The Battle of Austerlitz is one of the most wonderful moments of Napoleon's glory. Then, as in Italy, he defeated the enemy with inferior numbers by the mere force of his guns. When in the morning he saw the course the enemy's columns were taking, he rubbed his hands, and said to General Lannes, "I told you they would do what I desire." It was at Austerlitz that for the first time French *cuirassiers* charged the enemy's batteries.

Napoleon spent the night by himself after the battle wrapped in his blue overcoat, lying on a hard bench, and using his three-cornered hat as a pillow. At 5 a. m. he woke up and called out for his orderly, who slept on a bundle of straw outside his door. Receiving no reply, he went out and found him still fast asleep. "Wake up, Savey," he said, gently shaking the soldier; "everyone must rise, we must go our rounds. Go and wake the staff officers who are to accompany me." Savey, in a dream, jumped up, touched by not having been reprimanded by his emperor, and hastened to do his bidding. The emperor in the meantime walked about to get some warmth, as the weather was bitterly cold.

The moon was shining brightly, and from its light he perceived a little way off a grenadier sentinel, an old soldier, who, knowing that military honours need not be given to officers at that time in the morning, stood at ease with his gun between his legs, and in the emperor's presence quietly proceeded to fill a broken pipe with tobacco. The emperor called out to him: "One may say it is very cold this morning."

"Certainly it was much warmer yesterday during the fire of the battle," the grenadier replied, blowing his fingers, and continued: "You had a famous plan yesterday when you drove them into a hole to give them a hot bath of cannon-balls. I think it has been a lesson for them which will teach them politeness another time."

"Sire," said Savey, who had joined the emperor during this short dialogue, "this soldier speaks the truth. Your Majesty has never been so well inspired and never has your army shown more valour."

"They desired war," Napoleon replied, continuing his walk before the hut; "I have only paid them out; but we must act honourably and mercifully to the end. There must still be many of them wounded on the battlefield." Sire, the enemy suffered." We will now go and see to this ourselves," and then, turning abruptly to the orderly, added: "These people had nothing to do but to swallow us up if they had been more clever in their tactics."

"Yes, yes," the soldier replied, "but *we* crossed their line."

This sharp reply made the emperor laugh, then, calling up his escort, he mounted his charger and rode away to the battlefield, and there began his long review of the dead and wounded, his own and the enemy's. He had enjoined silence on his escort, so that the moans of the wounded might not miss his ear.

Many times he dismounted and poured out a glass of brandy from the supply they had taken with them, and gave it to the wounded men to drink. He had all the dead covered with rugs, and stretchers were brought up for the wounded. He ordered fires to be lighted near each wounded man, and words of gratitude were poured on him from those who yesterday had been his enemies. He did not leave the field for many hours, and when he did, he left some of his suite with orders to remain there till the last wounded man was conveyed to the hospital. On his way back Napoleon heard a cry of pain, and, looking round, saw a poor wounded soldier in a ditch, vainly trying to raise himself. Napoleon hastened to him, "Your name?" he asked him, with great gentleness.

"Jabalot, Sergeant of the Light Brigade, a Parisian promoted to the 4th Rank," the man replied, in a faint voice.

Napoleon called to one of his officers, "I charge you to see that this man is attended to immediately. You will have to answer for him to me."

"Do not trouble about me," said Jabalot; "it is not worth while disturbing yourselves—I am done for."

"I pray not," said the emperor; "one blow does not kill a Frenchman."

"Excuse me," said Jabalot, attempting to rise, "it was a clean shot."

"You have indeed been very brave; the Cross and the Order will be yours at the next review," said Napoleon, gently patting him on the shoulder.

"Alas, sire!" Jabalot answered, in a very weak voice, "I am dying; but one sergeant more or less in the regiment, what does that matter? Promotion for others, that is all. It will not prevent the 4th Regiment marching fearlessly to the battle with fixed bayonets, and being always invincible."

Napoleon bade him a tender farewell, and again ordering his *aide-de-camp* to do all he could for the dying man, sadly mounted his horse and rode away. The next morning Napoleon's first thought was to send for the officer and to ask him news of Jabalot.

Sire," he replied, "he no longer suffers."

"Ah," said the emperor, with a deep sigh, striking his foot with his riding-whip several times, "you must go to the colonel of Jabalot's regiment and find out if he was married, and if he had children or any relatives, and bring me a written report of his services. Within two hours the 4th Regiment will be stationed at Brunn, so do not delay."

While the army was preparing for a further march. Napoleon and some cavalry officers took the road towards Austerlitz, as he wished to reconnoitre the country round from the various hills in the district. On reaching the town, he asked who was the owner of a large castle he observed perched on a high hill, and was told it belonged to the Prince Kaunitz. "It is well," he said; "I will sleep there tonight. Send the carriages on, gentlemen, with supplies," and he added gaily, "I will entertain you all there at Austria's expense, and rather better than you dine in the huts."

While all was getting ready at the castle, he rode on to Brunn, where several detachments of the army had arrived, and there he distributed many decorations and praised each recipient for his individual bravery. But on stopping in front of a battalion which had wavered before the pressure of a cavalry regiment of the Imperial Guard, a frown spread over his face, and, backing his horse some steps, his keen eyes wandered along the ranks, and he exclaimed, sharply, "Soldiers, what has become of the eagle which I gave you when you took the oath to defend the standard until death?"

A light murmur followed by the deepest silence was the only answer to this stern address. Then the colonel of the battalion stepped forward, holding his sword with its point to the ground, and, in a hesitating voice, said: "Sire, the standard-bearer was killed at the onset of the first charge, and it was only after the second that the regiment was able to reform itself, and we then perceived that our standard had disappeared."

"And what did you do without one," Napoleon asked, in a severe tone.

"Sire, we captured from the Russian *cuirassiers* a standard with a hooded eagle to offer to your Majesty in its place."

An officer then stepped up with the standard, and stood silently before the emperor. He gazed at the trophy for a moment, and then said, "Can you all swear to me on your honour that every effort was made to recover the eagle?"

Loud shouts of "Yes, Yes," resounded from the regiment.

"And will you swear zealously to guard the new flag I will give you? Remember that a soldier who loses his flag loses everything."

Another shout of "Yes" broke out.

"Then," said the emperor, "I will accept the enemy's trophy from you and bestow a new flag on the 4th Regiment."

Then, turning to the colonel, he continued, in a less severe tone than when he had first spoken to him, "Come and see me after the review; I have something to say to you."

The long inspection at length came to an end, and the colonel at once went to Napoleon's tent, greatly fearing some reprimand.

"Ah, ah, colonel, I am very glad to see you," was the emperor's greeting; then, drawing him aside, in a lower voice, he said, "How was it your regiment gave way in the last battle?"

"Sire, the enemy was so close to us, it was impossible for us to make a united charge."

"The usual pretext and excuse, evidently."

"Sire, it is not my fault if I am not killed," the colonel replied, with sarcasm.

"Ah, colonel, you are mistaken. God forbid that I should reproach you for being alive and well today. I only wished to remind you that it behoves you, colonel, and officers of the regiment, to give the example of courage to your soldiers, and lead them on."

"Sire," the poor colonel replied, with pale lips and sad eyes, "I do not think I showed any want of courage."

"Your soldiers were nervous, I tell you," repeated the emperor, raising his voice and looking at the colonel with stern eyes. "I understand all about it, and they are cowards and liars who can boast of *never* having been afraid at least once in their lives. Do you understand now?" Then, approaching the officer quietly, he noticed on the collar of his coat a hole. "What is that?" asked the emperor, with a smile full of interest, passing one of his fingers through it. "Here is a buttonhole which is not in the order for today."

"I don't know," replied the commander quietly.

"And this epaulet," continued Napoleon, always in the same tone.

"See what a state it is in. You require another."

In fact, half of the epaulet had been carried away by a bullet.

"Sire, perhaps it was a bullet," replied the officer, without seeming to attach any importance to these irrefutable proofs of his courage. "Yes, a bullet, which also made a hole; that's all!"

"One moment, you are in a great hurry," said the emperor, with impatience, striking the ground with the heel of his boot, as the colonel seemed to wish to retire, "I have still something more to say."

Then, poking his finger again in the hole, making it still bigger, he continued, "This evening. colonel, after the roll-call, and having inspected your men, you will go to Berthier, and you will tell him to give you a new epaulet. Now, be calm, and take care not to let yourself be killed, as you threatened to do. Your emperor loves you and appreciates you more than any one." And, having lightly pulled his moustache, he left him, doubtless to avoid a sentimental scene.

The victory of Austerlitz had been a thunderbolt for the enemies, according to Napoleon, for not only had it put an end to the campaign of 1805, but it also destroyed the Third Coalition formed against France. At Austerlitz the victory was complete. This was not the case in the Battle of Eylau, which Napoleon compared to an earthquake, and which the Russians maintained they had gained, while we declared we had never lost it. This battle was in reality one of the most terrible which the great army had yet fought. The whole morning passed in useless firing, according to Junot, who performed prodigies of valour there as elsewhere. Towards three o'clock in the afternoon, however, the engagement became so violent that the bravest were horrified. Two batteries of the Guard, composed of four companies of the 12th Division, under the orders of General Lariboissière, fired on the Russians without interval and annihilated them, till night put an end to the carnage and our army bivouacked on the battle-field in the position still held.

At daybreak Napoleon rode through the lines of the still sleeping soldiers, whom he would not allow to be awakened. The enemy's army had retreated for some miles, leaving the ground covered with dead, dying, and wounded. Napoleon, who always carried out his practice of looking after his enemy's wounded as if they were his own, rode over the ground and made a halt at every step, to comfort and help the suffering men. The zeal and efforts of Larry, Chief Army Surgeon, and that of his assistants in the Ambulance Corps, which he had organised, hardly sufficed for treating all the wounded, and the means of transporting them became nil. There were no more carriages or horses to be found in the ruined villages surrounding the battlefield.

Napoleon then issued an appeal to the wandering and homeless population, offering twenty *francs* to each person who would remove wounded men from the battlefield, and convey them to the hospitals. The sympathy of Napoleon, even more than the twenty *francs*, produced the desired effect. Men, women, old and young, hurried from all quarters, bringing wheelbarrows and small handcarts, and lost no time in carrying away the wounded. They were all eager to show their gratitude for Napoleon's care and kindness when they had only expected hatred and revenge.

On returning to his camp, the emperor rode over the ground on which sixteen French generals, among them d'Hautpoul, Dalhmann, and Corbineau were killed. On seeing them still lying there, in a low voice he murmured, "'What a heavy toll death has taken here." Shortly after a long procession of ambulances and stretchers bearing Russian corpses to their last resting-place passed him. As soon as he saw this funeral procession approaching, he pulled up his horse, and called to his staff, "Halt, gentlemen! Hats off!" and took off his own . "All honour to the brave and courageous," he said, and did not move till the last stretcher had gone by. A few minutes afterwards he saw a soldier carrying on his shoulder a shapeless mass. "Go and see what it is," he said to one of his staff. The officer swiftly obeyed him.

"Sire,'" he said, on his return, "it is a young drummer boy who is being taken to the hospital. He has lost both his legs."

"Poor boy," said the emperor, looking up to heaven as if a painful recollection had suddenly crossed his mind, then added, "Run, run, quickly, and ask his name and the number of his regiment."

The officer saluted and rode off. During his short absence, Napoleon seemed unable to master his great emotion. All who were present noticed it. The officer returned.

"Sire, it is a little drummer boy of the 4th Regiment of Artillery. His name is Sibert, he . . ."

"Oh, my God" cried the emperor, interrupting the messenger. "Enough, enough, I do not wish to know any more!"

He dropped his reins, and covered his face with both hands, saying in a broken voice, "Unhappy mother! Poor child! Oh, war, war!"' Then he went off at a gallop, his suite following him in silence.

On the evening before the battle, while reviewing the 4th Artillery Regiment, Napoleon had noticed little Sibert, who was scarcely twelve years old. He was drummer of the 1st battalion of this regiment. The emperor, surprised at his small stature, for he could hardly carry his drum, approached him smiling, and, patting him under the chin, said, "How old are you, little rogue?"

"Just twelve years old."

"They were wrong to send you here—they should have waited three or four years longer," said Napoleon. "Have you a father?"

"No, my emperor, he was killed at Austerlitz; it was my mother who wished it."

"You will tell your mother from me that she has no common sense. But they are all alike! What is your mother's surname?"

"Sibert, sire; she is *vivandière* to the 20th Regiment. She knows you very well, and so does my brother François."

"Ah, you have a brother! Doubtless he is with your mother?"

"Yes, my emperor, he is piper in the 20th Regiment, but he is older than I am."

"You will tell your mother that I said you were too young to be in the army. Fine soldiers, indeed, of your age to oppose Wittgenstein's *cuirassiers*."

"Oh, no," replied Sibert, standing on the points of his toes, "Monsieur Romeuf, our head drummer, gives me private lessons every day. Already I know all the tattooes."

"Oh, that is different!" replied Napoleon, with a smile of approbation. "Since Monsieur Romeuf, the head drummer, gives you private lessons, there is nothing else to say. We shall be able to judge tomorrow, both of his talent and of the progress that you have made under his teaching."

The emperor then went away laughing, imitating the manner of the little drummer.

Alas, the next day the brave boy kept his word. Beating his drum with the assurance of an old soldier, in the midst of a violent Russian attack on his regiment, a bullet shattered both knees, and he cried out, lying on the snow: "Arms up! Fire! Long live the emperor!". . . Then he said to an old sergeant in a lamentable voice, "Oh, my friend, do not leave me here tonight; they will kill me. Take me away, I beg you. Put me in a wagon of the 20th Regiment that I may be able to kiss my mother once more before I die." The soldier was just carrying him to a wagon when the emperor stopped him, recognising the boy, and had all care taken of him. Later on he was seen with the cross of the "*Legion d'Honneur*" on his breast, which Napoleon especially sent him.

"Berthier," said Napoleon one day, referring to the wounded and dying, "the heart speaks louder than politics; glory then loses all its illusion." Davoust, Marmont, and Macdonald were the heroes who were foremost in annihilating the Austrians, and who entered Vienna with their "Idol," but Lannes, Pouzet, Lasalle d'Espagne, and other famous men were the glorious heroes who lost their lives. It was as if Napoleon need only say, "Go," and they went; "Die," and they died.

One day he saw a general engaged in an unnecessary fight. Being found fault with by the emperor, he answered, "Sire, glory is like champagne, it goes to one's head."

"But the blood of the soldiers cannot be compared to wine, which is easily thrown out of the windows. You should, if necessary, spare your brave brigade," replied the emperor. "See what is left of it—only half."

"Enough for another time, sire."

"What a man!" said the emperor, as he rode away.

Napoleon won the affection of his soldiers in a thousand ways, and none of them ever murmured through all the horrors they had to face; that they were all for their emperor was enough recompense for them, and their pride was in being able in any way to help him to attain the glory for which he strove. It was in small things he so entered into their lives, as the following example proves. During the campaign in Austria the emperor's busy brain prevented him from sleeping, so, leaving his staff asleep, he rose and donned his grey overcoat, as it was bitterly cold and wet. He pulled up the large collar and put his hat well over his face, so as not to be recognised, and walked round one of the bivouacs, where the men were asleep by a wood fire, which was just smouldering, and on its ashes several potatoes were lying. The idea seized him to eat one of them, so with the point of his sword he scraped one out. At that moment one of the sleepers opened his eyes, and seeing, as he thought, a thief trying to steal their potatoes, he called out, without getting up. "Well, Mr. Sans Gêne, I beg you to leave our potatoes alone and go and look for your eatables elsewhere."

"Comrade," the emperor replied, turning his back to the soldier, for fear he should recognise him, "I am desperately hungry, will you not let me have a little one?"

"Ah, that is different when you ask like that, and if you are so hungry, take one and even two, but hurry up; we shall soon be called, and you must be off, as you have no business here," and seeing the emperor did not hasten to move, he added, "Don't let me have to tell you again, or I shall lose my temper."

Napoleon continued calmly to move the cinders, then the soldier, losing patience, rose and flung himself on the marauder, and was just seizing him by the throat when Napoleon turned his head, pushed up his hat, and was recognised. How can one depict the shame and mortification of the grumbler! He fell at Napoleon's feet, exclaiming, "Oh, my emperor, I am a wretch—I deserve to die!"

"Hush!" the emperor said; "you will wake up your comrades, who need sleep. I am not angry. It is I who am to blame for touching your potatoes."

"Oh, my emperor, take them all! See here, sire, here is a splendid one," and the soldier began picking one out of the still hot cinders.

"You will burn your hands; leave the potatoes alone—I am no longer hungry."

Then the soldier caught hold of the tail of Napoleon's coat and kissed it, until he said: "There, there, that's enough, let me go, or I shall be angry." Then he added in a low voice, "I forgive you. Be happy now and in the future, and whatever you do, do not talk of this to anyone." He then returned to his tent.

A few days afterwards, during one of his inspections after a battle, the emperor saw a soldier approaching him in a most extraordinary mixture of garments. He walked with a limping step, his head was bound up with bandages, which gave him the appearance of a Mameluke, over his shoulder hung a cape, richly embroidered, which must have belonged to an Austrian officer, and he wore a pair of large, white linen trousers, drawn in tight at the ankles. "Who are you in this masquerade costume?" the emperor asked, with a frown, pulling up his horse.

"My emperor," giving the military salute, "here I am once more."

"Ah, ah," said the emperor, "but that does not answer my question, what is your name?"

"Do you not remember me, my emperor?"

"How could I recognise any one in motley clothes like yours?"

"That is true, I must resemble a Turk. It is my rascally comrades who disguised me like this, after tying my head up tight for fear it should fall to pieces, but I was determined to come and see you instead of going to the hospital, feeling sure it would do me more good, Already I feel better."

"I am delighted, but still you do not tell me who you are."

"I am the potato man," the soldier said, in a mysterious tone; "you remember, sire, some days ago, the potatoes, and I, I—"

"Oh, it is you, is it, and you have been badly wounded in the head?"

"Oh, it is nothing, just three bullets; at first I thought I was done for, but there, I am still alive to fight for you. My comrades gave me a good share of their brandy to strengthen me, sire, so as to see you."

The emperor was much touched, and kindly asked the soldier what reward he would like from him for his bravery—would he like money? The man shook his head. "An advance in rank?"

"No, sire, I am too old for that; I have been fighting for thirteen years. What I desire is—is . . ."

"Speak out, my man, I am in a hurry—speak."

"Well, sire, it is a medal of honour I so want," lifting his head up proudly, "in memory of all the great battles I have fought in—Austerlitz, Eylau, Jena . . ."

"There, there," said the emperor, "you have deserved it, and you shall have it today; you must go at once to the hospital and be well cared for, or else you may have no chance of wearing it," and the emperor rode away, while the soldier's eyes were streaming with gratitude as he walked slowly to the hospital murmuring to himself, "To think I refused him a potato!"

These are instances of how Napoleon won his soldiers' devotion.

Soldat d'artillerie légère et Vélites.
GARDE IMPÉRIALE.

Le Prince EUGÈNE, Colonel-général, commandant en chef les chasseurs à cheval (les Guides).
GARDE IMPÉRIALE.

CHAPTER 12

Incognito Wanderings

One of Napoleon's favourite diversions, which often gave him most amusing moments, was to go about Paris in disguise, like the celebrated Sultan in the *Arabian Nights*. His *grand vizier* was Duroc, who always accompanied him. Napoleon usually left the Tuileries before daylight by a small garden gate, of which he alone had the key, laughingly saying he was escaping from his 'prison' of the Tuileries. He wore for these excursions either a dark grey or blue overcoat, well buttoned over his chest, and a very large soft hat, which he could pull over his face. Duroc wore the same costume. Thus disguised, they wandered through the streets of the metropolis. Napoleon, with his eagle eye, taking note of any spot where improvements could be made in the principal streets and of what was needed in the houses of the poor to ameliorate the inmates' condition. Duroc had a book with him, in which all was transcribed.

He often visited the market in the early morning, and bought various things from the women, giving them a false address where to send them, at the same time slipping a gold piece into their hands and refusing change, leaving them mystified as to who their generous buyer could be. He was always on the lookout to relieve the poor. One day, on his way back to the palace, he saw an old gardener digging hard in one of the many public gardens in Paris; he went up to him, and said: "What do you earn a day, my friend?"

At these words the old man looked up, doffed his cap, and said: "Forty-five *sous* a day, sir."

"That is very little! Have you worked here for long, and what is your name?"

"Père Olivier, at your service, sir, and I worked in the gardens of the Petit Trianon in their blessed Majesties' reign. They often addressed kind words to me; may God have mercy on their souls," he said reverently.

"Poor man, poor man," said the emperor, "here are 200 *francs* for you to carry on with till I see you again."

"O God, is it possible!" cried Père Olivier, transported with joy at this unexpected gift. "Surely you must be one of the emperor's gentlemen. How is he, the brave man?"

"Very well, and I will speak to him of you."

"Really! Oh, the brave emperor! How I should like to see him before I die; but I fear there is little chance of that, as I am too old to go into crowds."

"How do you know you have not already seen him, without recognising him? Have you never been in a battle?"

"Yes, sir, years ago, in the last battles of Louis XV."

"You must have seen and heard many things during your life."

"Indeed, yes. Many times I saw the king with Madame Dubarry, and they often spoke to me just as I am talking to you. You, of course, never knew them; you are too young."

"That is true, but I have heard about it all."

"I now only busy myself with my work, so long as I can do that well. Politics are nothing to me. I have always been on the moderate side and do not bother myself about the government."

"You are quite right, and I know many people who would like to do the same. *Adieu*, my good man, I will see you again," and Napoleon, with a happy smile, continued his walk to the Tuileries.

Shortly afterwards, Père Olivier received a summons to go to the palace, where he was informed Napoleon had settled 500 *francs* a year on him, and what filled his heart with still more joy was that he saw his benefactor as he mounted his horse in the courtyard of the Tuileries.

Sometimes the emperor sallied forth in the evenings, while the shops were still open, so as to visit them and try to gather from the owners what they thought of him. One evening he went to a jeweller in the Rue Richelieu, and, having made some purchases, asked the jeweller what he thought of "that fool Napoleon." The jeweller, thinking from this question (he himself being an Imperialist), that he had to do with a Jacobin spy, seized a long broom from the corner of the shop and prepared to hit him for speaking in such terms of the emperor. Duroc hastened to interfere, begging that his friend might be forgiven, as he had spoken in a state of excitement, and they slipped away, the man shaking his fist at them. Napoleon, when at a safe distance, shook with laughter at having been chased out of a shop with a broom.

Another amusing adventure befell the *incognitoes* in the early hours of one morning. After a long walk through the town to see how the improvements were proceeding, they passed by a small *café* which was just opening. "Ah, Duroc, what a good thing; I am very thirsty. Let us go in and have some breakfast. This long walk has given me an appetite."

"Sir, it is too early; it is only just 8 o'clock."

"Nonsense, nonsense, your watch is always slow. I am famishing, and it will economise time for the rest of the day," and without waiting for Duroc's reply, he entered the *café*, called a *garçon*, and ordered mutton cutlets and omelette and some wine of Chambertin for two. He ate heartily and greatly praised the *café noir*, which he said was far better than what he had at the palace. Then he bade Duroc call the *garçon* and pay the account while he went outside, and stood in his usual attitude, with his hands behind his back, and gently whistled an Italian air.

Duroc in the meantime was in a predicament, as he found to his dismay that in the hurry of the early rising that morning he had forgotten his purse. He knew that Napoleon had nothing, as on his way there, with his usual generosity, he had given fifteen *louis*, all he had with him, to a workman in whom he had recognised a soldier who had bravely fought in the Prussian war, and who had been decorated by him, and finding in talking to him that he and his family were badly off, he at once emptied his purse. When the *garçon* gave Duroc the account, which amounted to twelve *francs*, and found that he had no money, he went and fetched his mistress, who angrily demanded the sum. Duroc replied gently, "*Madame*, my friend and I went out before daybreak this morning, and in our hurry we forgot our purses, but I give you my word of honour that on our return home I will at once send you what we owe."

"It may be true, sir," replied the angry dame, "but I do not know you or your friend, and every day one gets taken in. Surely you can understand."

Just then Napoleon came in, sayings "Hurry up! Why this delay?—it is getting late." But, at a sign from Duroc he guessed what had occurred, and drew his hat low over his face and went out to await the sequel of events, while Duroc said: "*Madame*, you need not fear, I give you my word we are honest men and form part of the palace guard."

The *garçon* on hearing this, and being sharper than his mistress, while she was asserting, with her arms *akimbo*, that they should not leave without payment, slipped away for a few moments, and on returning made a sign to Duroc, handed his mistress twelve *francs* out of his pocket, then gave it her, saying, "*Madame*, I will lend you the twelve *francs*, feeling sure that this gentleman will not wrong a poor boy like me."

She accepted it, grumbling at the bad habit of people ordering things without having money to pay for them.

Duroc, much touched, took out his watch and put it into the *garçon's* hands and bade him keep it as security for the money he had lent; but the boy absolutely refused to accept it, saying: "Sir, I have no need of securities; I feel sure you are both honest people."

"Yes, my friend, you will have no reason to repent of your confidence," replied Duroc, and with a bow to the angry *patronne*, he joined the emperor in the street.

The emperor laughed heartily, and greatly praised the boy, saying: "That boy is a true son of Paris; they are all impulsive and kind-hearted, giving away anything they have, right and left, without thought and without regard, but we owe him many thanks. Be sure and return his loan and add 100 *francs* to it without delay.

On their way back to the palace they passed through the Rue de la Paix, where new houses were being built. It was nine o'clock and many shops were not opened, which made the emperor exclaim: "These Parisians are indeed lazy, not having their shops open at this hour." As he went along he took note of everything, and of the alterations to be carried out by his architects.

In a side street, not far from the palace, in a shop where the shutters had been taken down, a pair of beautiful Medici vases, among a lot of other china, caught Napoleon's eye. He went in to ask the price, but no one was visible except a maid, who was busy dusting in. such an awkward way that the emperor could not help laughing, and said to her: "Is there no master or mistress? If there are, they must be a lazy couple not to be up yet."

"Do you wish to buy anything?" the maid asked in a grumbling tone, and, stopping her work, looked at the emperor, with her arms *akimbo*.

"Yes," he replied, "I want to know the price of these vases."

"Well, I should never have believed it from your appearance. I will ring up *madame.*" And, seizing a large hand-bell, she rang it with energy enough to rouse the whole neighbourhood, and *madame* soon appeared, half dressed, with a shawl hastily thrown over her shoulders.

"What can you want at this hour of the morning," she asked, in an angry voice.

"*Madame*, what is the price of these two vases?"

"Do you want to buy them, sir?"

"Evidently," said the emperor, in a tone of surprise.

"Four thousand *francs*; not one *sou* less."

"Four thousand *francs!*" exclaimed the emperor, the tone and the manner of the woman displeasing him. "Far too high a price for me, *madame*," and was going out of the shop when the woman placed herself in his way, and with her hands on her hips, said:

"But they are worth more than that; I gave five thousand *francs* for them, but it is better to sell at a loss than not at all; if we did not do so we should die of hunger, such a bad state all is in now. Always war, war, war. Everyone is complaining. Business is bad all round. Trades people are ruined with all the heavy taxes and payments."

During this tirade the physiognomy of the emperor took an expression impossible to describe, turning from red to a deep pallor, the muscles of his face contracted, his lips became blue, and his eyes sparkled with anger. He crossed his arms over his chest, and said:

"Have you a husband, *madame?*" in the sharp voice which always impressed any one he was addressing. "Where is he? Why does he not come down?"

"Ah, ha, do not get in such a rage, sir. Yes, God be thanked, I have one and a good one; he has been out since daybreak to try and make a little money—some that is owing to him; precious difficult in these times to get money. No one has a penny. But why do you want him? Am not I here?"

"Enough, enough, *madame*, I wish to tell your husband that perhaps, later on, I might think of the vases—later on, I will see."

Napoleon, more ashamed of his anger than of that of the woman, joined Duroc, who was waiting outside, and said: "Well, I have had a sermon today. A woman, a stupid woman, troubling herself over politics when she ought to be occupying herself with her business. Her husband must be a fool to allow it," and he continued talking like this till he reached the palace in a state of agitation.

So it happened to him sometimes, as to others, to have illusions destroyed.

The next morning a servant in the emperor's livery appeared at the *café*, and said to its mistress: "*Madame*, is it not here that yesterday two gentlemen came and had breakfast and had no money with them?"

"Yes, sir! " the woman replied in surprise, at seeing the royal servant.

"Well, *madame*, they were the emperor and his Grand Marshal Duroc. Can I speak to the *garçon* who waited on them?"

"Certainly, but—sir—" *Madame* rang for the *garçon* all in a tremble, and said she would drown herself if not allowed to throw herself at the emperor's feet to implore his pardon, and could not believe her eyes when the servant put into the *garçon's* hands 112 *francs*, saying to him, "The grand marshal sends you this from His Majesty, the Emperor, and also I am to tell you you are to be engaged as footman at the palace and will form part of the Empress Josephine's retinue. I will come and fetch you tomorrow. As to you, *madame*, you are forgiven."

The *garçon* remained with Josephine till her divorce, when she retired to Malmaison, and, singular destiny of those days, he ended by entering Lord Wellington's service in 1814.

Another official went to the china shop and said to the proprietor: "Sir, I am sent by the emperor to order you to come with me at once to the palace and bring with you the two vases his Majesty looked at the other day. Hurry up! The emperor doesn't like waiting."

"Oh, my God! "he exclaimed, "am I to be shot?" Then, addressing his wife, who looked stupefied, he continued: "I see it all. You abused the government as you do every day, and to whom? His Majesty, the Emperor! Will you never keep your wicked tongue in order? How often have I told you to do so? And you took him for an impostor! Oh, my God, all is over, and I shall be sent to prison!"

Terror quite took away the poor man's senses, though Napoleon's servant did all he could to reassure him. At last he recovered sufficiently to take up the vases and get into the fiacre which was waiting to drive him to the Tuileries.

On arriving there he was at once ushered into the emperor's presence, but trembled so he could hardly stand. "Ah, ah, sir, I see you at last," the emperor said, in a stern tone, though he had a great desire to laugh. "Now let me look again at the vases." Having examined these carefully, he took out of his purse 8,000 *franc* notes and handed them to the trembling and astonished man, who hardly understood he was meant to take them, till the emperor spoke again: "I went to your shop the other day and asked the price of these vases. Your wife asked

4,000 *francs* for them, saying she had paid 5,000. So, take these notes of 8,000. There are 4,000 *francs* for the vases. Your wife, of course, told a lie when she said she had given 5,000. The extra 4,000 are to make up for the anger your wife caused me to show, for speaking so ill, as she did, of the government. Tell her never again to mix herself up in politics or you will both find yourselves in prison. There, sir, you can go. I have nothing more to say."

Soldat Crétillois Infra et Voltron.

GARDE IMPÉRIALE.

Officier de la garde de la Convention et Soldat de la garde du Directoire (à cheval).

GARDE IMPÉRIALE.

CHAPTER 13

A Night at Provins

A good lady, bent with age, who lived in a small house at Provins, told me the following story.

"In February, 1814, when several battles had taken place not very far from the town, I had to put up many soldiers, but for a few days the house was empty and I was occupied in putting it in order, when my servant, one dark evening, came to tell me that an officer had arrived and was to be billeted on me.

"I went to receive him, and a short man entered, rather stout, with a sallow complexion and dark hair flat on his head, wearing a grey coat over his uniform which hid his decorations and epaulettes, so it was impossible to see what rank he held in the army. He apologised for the intrusion, but I could not help showing that I was vexed at his coming so suddenly, and I asked him whence he came.

"He replied: 'From Bray-sur-Seine!'

"' Oh, in that case,' I said, 'you must have taken part in the battle, where I have been told the Emperor of Russia and the King of Prussia were nearly taken prisoners, so come in and relate to me what took place.'

"'With pleasure.' he replied, and sitting down he gave me a full description of the battlefield and of the position that each corps of the French Army occupied so as to cut off the retreat of the Allies, and he ended by asking if I had ever seen the emperor.

"'I only saw him once when he was general of the Italian Army, and certainly should not recognise him.'

"'Well, look well at me; I am told I much resemble him. I, in fact, never leave him; no one, unless in his shirt, can ever be so like him as I am.'

"'And, sir, where are you going to now?'

"'I am going to Paris; if I say to *créer des cadres*, I suppose you would not understand me.'

"'What do you mean when you say you never leave the emperor, and yet you are here and talking of going to Paris?'

"'That is true, but all the same there are occasions—'

"'Oh, just a moment. Have you a certificate for a lodging or any papers to show me? You know we are not allowed to put up soldiers unless their papers are in order.'

"'In that case, *madame*, you must send me away, as I have neither certificate nor papers.'

"'Oh, no, I will take the risk. I cannot turn you out on a dark night like this, and no one else would take you in; besides, you can tell me a lot of things. Are the Cossacks likely to return here?'

"'Alas, you must not trust to their not doing so,' he said, with a sigh. 'We are not getting sufficient support. If only,' he continued, smiling, 'all the women would turn out and fight, we should soon defeat the Allies—' but at this moment a violent knock at the outside door made me tremble, and, getting up, I cried: 'Oh, my God, it is, perhaps, the Cossacks! Oh, my poor home, it will be pillaged!'

"The officer came to me and, taking my two old hands in his, said, very gently: 'Be calm, *madame*; it is most likely some one who wishes to speak to me.' So it was; the door was thrown open, and my servant ushered in two officers in uniform, who said they wished to speak to their '*commandant*.' The *commandant* (that was what my officer was), who was seated by the fire, remained in his chair and made a sign to the officers, putting his finger on his lips as if to warn them to speak low, or not to speak at all; then, without rising, he said to them:

"'Sirs, salute *madame* and crave her forgiveness for coming here without an invitation.' The officers made me a graceful bow, and, to do honour to my guests, I hastened to light two more candles. After a few whispered words between the three, the new arrivals (one of whom was a remarkably handsome and distinguished-looking man) departed. I then offered to get supper for my visitor, but he said he would wait and have it with me at my usual hour.

"'In that case,' I said, 'you will wait for ever, for I very seldom have supper, still less this evening, as I am not feeling very well, but I have a fine chicken which I will roast for you, and as the Cossacks may be returning, I would rather a Frenchman ate it than one of them.'

"'Oh, a chicken!' he cried. 'Why, *madame*, that is luxury; a few potatoes cooked on cinders is all that a soldier needs.'

"I then asked him if he had any servants with him. 'No, *madame*, I am alone. It is too sad that we have to live on the poor inhabitants of villages who take us in, but, *madame*,' he continued, 'as you are so gracious to me, will you grant me a favour, which is that you will honour me by supping with me at this table.'

"'Sir, I will do whatever you wish,' I replied. While my servant laid the table, I cooked the chicken, but still kept talking to my visitor. I spoke to him of the emperor, and of all the admiration I had for him, and said he was a hero, and added that I had seen the King of Prussia. Here he interrupted me, saying: 'Madame, I hope you are not going to compare Napoleon to him.' This, of course, I absolutely denied, but said I blamed the emperor for not being quiet, and that I could not understand why he was not contented with being Emperor of the French and the first sovereign in the world.

"The *commandant* listened to me smilingly, balancing himself in his chair. I got so excited in the conversation that at moments I forgot the chicken and walked about the room. 'But, *madame*,' he said, rising from his chair, and taking my hand, 'calm yourself; good God, you are impetuous! The emperor has many things to reproach himself with: the first is to have gorged his generals with gold, the second to have divorced Josephine, and the third to have married an Austrian.'

"'If the Prussians come here, I shall fly from them,' I said.

"'Do not do anything so foolish, for you would then lose everything. I know all about it, *madame*, so follow my advice. You have this nice house; always ask to have officers billeted on you in preference to their men, and your property will be respected.'

"The table had been laid; the chicken was cooked, and with some boiled eggs, salad, bread, butter and wine, the supper made quite a respectable appearance. While we were eating, he kept saying: 'God, what a good chicken! I have never eaten a better one. I drink to your good health, *madame*.'

"At ten he begged to go to bed, so I conducted him to a bedroom which had been got ready. He insisted on carrying the candle and offered me his hand, and on entering his room, exclaimed: 'What a good fire! What a nice looking bed! It is long since I have been so comfortable; I shall indeed sleep well.'

"He then shook me warmly by the hand, thanking me for all I had done for him, and said he would bid me *adieu* then, as he had to leave very early in the morning, and did not want me to be disturbed. I bade him goodnight, and retired to bed.

"When my servant got up at 5 a. m. the next morning, she saw the *commandant* walking up and down outside the house, with his arms crossed behind his back.

"A few days afterwards I lodged a colonel, to whom I related all this, and he then informed me I had lodged the emperor himself! No such idea had ever entered my head, and I was dumbfounded to think of all I had said. Shortly afterwards I received his portrait signed by himself, which is my most treasured possession."

Le Grenadier de l'île d'Elbe.
GARDE IMPÉRIALE.

CHAPTER 14

Small Gifts Cement Friendships

The way in which gifts are made is often more valuable than the gifts themselves. This axiom was fully justified by Napoleon, who possessed in the highest degree the knack of enhancing the value of the smallest gift he made by his gracious manner in bestowing it. His voice on these occasions became tender and caressing, his eyes sparkled with kindness, and his smile often reassured kings when crowns seemed tottering after his great victories.

At the same time, the emperor was by no means a spendthrift. The house expenses were overlooked with rigid severity. The smallest sums spent had to be accounted for. A mistake in the entry of a few *francs* drew grave reproaches on the House Steward, but although, like Sully, he looked at every penny in small things, on important occasions he never gave a thought as to what he spent on a gift. Josephine often chaffed him on his *"bouffées de générosité."* Napoleon maliciously replied, "Yes, yes, laugh at me as much as you like. It is all very well for you to do so, when you like to burn the candle at both ends at the same time, and to burn it quicker, you light it in the middle."

"All the same," replied Josephine, "you are often more extravagant than I am in your so-called small gifts; I can prove this to you if you wish."

At these words Napoleon laughed gaily, and rubbing his hands, said: "It is quite possible, but, *mon Dieu*, I know what I am about; I have my reasons. *Small gifts cement friendships.*"

This popular motto was his excuse for his, at times, over-profuse generosity. Everyone knows the mania Napoleon had for making marriages, and with what promptitude all was arranged. Unfortunately, they did not all turn out as well as might be wished, although he never failed to settle a handsome sum on the happy pair. His special gift to the bride was offered with the tact and delicacy which always distinguished his private affairs. On the occasion of the marriage of one of his favourite *aides-de-camp*, the evening before the wedding. Napoleon, after having given him the password for the night, laughingly said, "Now, I hope you do not forget that you are going to be married tomorrow."

"Certainly not, sire."

"Well, I give you a holiday of twenty-four hours, but after that your service with me must be renewed. You will then present your wife to me. Ah, I had almost forgotten her! (taking from the table a beautiful bouquet of artificial flowers). Give her this gift from me; it is my wedding present. You can tell her one of her great friends has sent it, and you will explain that if he did not select real flowers, it was only that they should last longer. Now, goodnight, and tell the administrator of the heating apparatus that it is all working very badly, and if it is not better tomorrow, he will be severely reprimanded."

The next day the bride, after admiring the wonderful delicacy of the bouquet composed of white lilies, which might well be mistaken for real ones, undid the paper, and found in its folds a most beautiful chain, composed of a large number of fine pearls, alternated with diamonds, rubies, and emeralds. The officer was less touched by this beautiful gift to his bride than by the words of the evening before: "Tell your wife that it is a gift from one of her best friends."

Napoleon, however, was stingy in his gifts to members of his household. He never gave them presents; they could therefore only count on their salaries, which, however, at times of war were often augmented if they had been travelling with him in any of the campaigns; but if these augmentations were given, the emperor expected that their clothes should do credit to their salaries. It is really extraordinary to think that the master of half Europe should occupy himself with the dress of one of his head servants, but he did so, to such a point that, seeing one of them in the same clothes for three days running, he said to him, angrily, "You look very untidy today, have you been ill?" On the other hand, if he saw one in a new suit, well made and in good taste, he would stop in front of him and say, with a smile, "Sir, how well you are turned out today. That is quite right, and that is how I like to see you."

At the time of his marriage with Marie Louise, and on the birth of the King of Rome, none of his household received gifts, as the emperor found that the expenses for these two festivities had gone far beyond what he had estimated.

He often acted on the spur of the moment, and gave gifts when least expected. On his birthday, 1812, Napoleon suddenly turned round to his head valet, Constant, who was dressing him, and said: "Constant, always wait on me as you do now, I will always look after you. You have got a bad cough. Take three rolls of barley sugar; they are an excellent remedy, and will do you good. I always use them." Then, putting on his hat, he left the room without waiting for Constant's thanks, who was more touched by his master's solicitude for his cough than for the rolls of barley sugar. However, he thought he would try one, but on unwrapping one of the rolls, he found three 40-*franc* pieces in each, wrapped in a 1,000-*franc* note.

I do not know whether these small details of Napoleon's life will interest any one, but anyhow, they show how he acted with regard to his household, and give fresh insight into his private character. Also it shows that the strict economy with which he managed his affairs in private life enabled him to act generously when it was helpful to others.

Napoleon's impatient disposition never brooked delay in anything he decided on, and he liked every one to be under his hand. One evening, for instance, after working for some time with Réal, his Councillor of State, he suddenly said to him: "The house where you live is eight *lieues* from Paris; that is too far. At any moment I may want you. I cannot go on sending for you that distance; you must at once buy another one nearer Paris."

"Sire, I cannot buy another house before I sell this one. Your Majesty knows well one cannot get rid of property at a moment's notice."

"You do not understand me, my dear friend; I do not want you to hurry over the sale, I merely say you must buy another. I well understand that after your work here all day, you need rest and distraction with your family, and good air, one or two *lieues* from Paris, but you can understand that if I want you in a hurry, that is quite far enough for you to be; therefore, it is essential you should at once buy another house."

"Sir, I quite understand all your Majesty says, but to buy, money is needed."

"Well, sir, do you not receive a large salary?"

"Sire, I am fully sensible of your Majesty's generosity, but with a family one cannot put by much."

"You are wrong. Do as you like, arrange whatever suits you, but you must be near me at once; something must be arranged by the day after tomorrow. That is my decisive order."

The next day, before the work began, Napoleon said, "Well, have you found a house, and have you sold yours?"

"Sire, buyers are needed for selling and money for buying; I will take rooms in Paris in the meantime, so as to be near your Majesty. Your Majesty knows well we no longer live in the old times, when properties could be had for nothing."

"That is true. Go on seeking; often opportunities occur when least expected for buying and selling."

The next morning Réal received an envelope from the emperor, enclosing a draft for 400,000 *francs*, to be spent entirely on a house near Paris. It is thus that Réal was able to become possessor of the beautiful property, in the Bois de Boulogne, now belonging to M. le Baron Rothschild.

Often the emperor quietly helped officers in his army, and manufacturers who for want of money could not carry on their business, also many cases of distress in Paris of which he heard, as he always gave instructions that all genuine cases should be reported to him. A poor senator died suddenly, to whom the emperor had advanced 100,000 *francs*, and for which sum the emperor held his note of hand, as he had lent him the money out of his Privy Purse; the day after his death he tore up the receipt, so that no claim should ever be made on the relatives.

Two more accounts of gifts from the emperor, one of which to Talma, the great actor, will close this chapter. He had summoned him to the Tuileries to consult with him as to the production of a tragedy at the *Théâtre Français*, in which he was to have the principal part. The discussion, which lasted for half an hour, being over, Napoleon showed him a magnificent antique cameo, which he had received from Italy, the head of a Roman emperor, of most admirable workmanship.

"What do you think of it?" he asked him.

"It is most beautiful, sire."

"Look at it carefully. Do you see anything particular in it?"

"Sire, in looking at it carefully, I think the profile greatly resembles your Majesty."

"That is so, and I am delighted that you see the resemblance, because the cameo as a jewel would have been a trifle I should not have asked you to accept. As a portrait, it is a souvenir that perhaps you will deign to accept from me," and he then added as usual his favourite maxim, "*Small gifts cement friendships.*"

A few years afterwards. Napoleon, forgotten at St. Helena, begged Count Bertrand to exchange his watch with him, and he knew in doing so that it would be a souvenir of glory for his grand marshal. "Remember, Bertrand," he said, "this watch struck 2 a.m. at Rivoli when I ordered Joubert to make an attack."

These are the ways in which the emperor bestowed gifts.

Officier porte-drapeau des Grenadiers à pied, et Grenadier à pied, grande tenue.
GARDE IMPÉRIALE.

Chasseur à pied, grande tenue d'hiver, et Officier des grenadiers à pied en petite tenue.
GARDE IMPÉRIALE.

CHAPTER 15

The Ball and the Fire

In the early days of June, 1810, on the return of Napoleon and Marie Louise from Belgium, where they had been travelling, a delayed series of festivities took place in Paris in honour of their marriage. The three most remarkable of them were those given by the City of Paris at the Hôtel de Ville, the second by the officers of the army at the Military School, and the third by Prince Schwartzenberg, the Ambassador of Austria, at the embassy in the Rue de Provence. Alas, this magnificent ball ended in a terrible catastrophe! It was fixed for the first Sunday in July. Invitations were sent out to everyone of distinction in Paris, including the King of Saxony, the Grand Duke and Duchess of Würtemberg and all the Imperial Highnesses, and to many illustrious foreigners who happened to be in Paris.

Nothing was left undone by the ambassador to make the ball worthy of the daughter of his sovereign. Over two thousand persons of rank were present. An enormous ball-room had been erected in the garden, constructed of wood, connected with the embassy by passages trellised with flowers. Its walls were covered with beautiful brocades, and festoons of silver gauze hung from the roof. On each side of one of the principal entrances floated flags with the arms of Austria and France cleverly intertwined. In order to prevent a crush on arriving, several entrances had been made, and nothing was left undone to avoid accident.

In the evening a company of the *Vieille garde* took possession of the embassy, as it was the etiquette that when the emperor went to a theatre or to any entertainment, they should be on the spot, and those selected were always the tallest and finest of the battalion. The ball was preceded by a great diplomatic dinner, at which all the ambassadors and foreign ministers were present. At nine o'clock crowds began to arrive, and the line of carriages became so thick they could hardly make their way through the multitudes who thronged the streets. One special route was kept clear for the royalties. Many people alighted from their carriages and walked. An amusing incident occurred to the King of Saxony, who, with his *aide-de-camp,* made his way on foot to the entrance reserved for royalties, but an old sentinel, when his name was given, cried out: "No, no, the general public do not come in this way! A king, you say? No, no! More than thirty kings have already entered, and there can be no more of them. Retire!—retire!" Fortunately the guard inside the entrance heard the altercation, and, recognising the king, rescued him from the overzeal of the old hussar.

From the description given by those who were present at this *fête,* the scene must indeed have been one of fairyland. The gardens were illuminated with thousands of coloured lights and the ballroom was like an enchanted bower. The whole room was filled with flowers of every colour and perfume, and the blaze of light from myriads of wax candles in crystal chandeliers, which reflected the light ten-fold, added to the rich dresses and jewels worn by the ladies and the brilliant uniforms of the kings, princes, ambassadors, and officers from all the courts in Europe, was a sight never to be forgotten.

The clock struck ten; trumpet and bugle announced the arrival of the emperor and empress. All the company stood up in line down the huge ballroom. The Austrian Ambassador, accompanied by his family and many civilians of high rank, had already gone to the embassy entrance to meet them, and accompanied them to the room. The emperor and Marie Louise stopped and spoke to their special friends and to the most illustrious guests as they passed; then the emperor led the empress to the throne erected at one end of the room and left her in company with the ambassadress and her ladies. She was expecting a child, and in view of the importance of the event to the country, though its date was still far distant, she was not allowed to take part in the dancing.

The emperor linked his arm in that of the King of Saxony to begin what he called his *tournée.* He was in a very good humour, and laughed heartily over the king's adventure at the entrance. They wandered all through the embassy rooms and gardens, admiring in detail the beautiful and allegorical devices that had been erected in their honour. The emperor had a kind word for everyone he passed, granted favours to various people, scolded the young men who were not dancing, and made sly remarks on the happy couples they caught sight of in various corners of the garden, busily engaged in flirting. They then returned to the ballroom to watch the dancing, which was proceeding gaily, but the heat in the room was very great, though all the windows had been thrown wide open, so the emperor returned to the garden, and numbers of guests followed his example.

What was the horror of all when about midnight, instead of trumpets sounding for supper, a cry of "Fire!—fire!" was heard. Many rushed out into the garden. The emperor's officers found him at some distance from the house in a little arbour, and rapidly told him what had occurred. "Gentlemen," he exclaimed in horror, "follow me!" and precipitately they flew to the ballroom, where the flames had already gained ground at one end. Pressing through the crowd, he reached the throne, took Marie Louise in his arms (who, with her ladies, had not realised at her end of the crowded room what had occurred), and carried her into the garden. The carriages having been called up, he bade the empress and her ladies drive to St. Cloud, where the court was then in residence.

He then returned to the sad scene. The fire had originated from a breath of wind through one of the ballroom windows wafting some of the gauze drapery over a chandelier, the candles of which at once set light to it. It seemed a small affair at first, and Prince Berthier rushed forward to tear down the drapery, but it tore in half, and the fire spread rapidly from one festoon to the other. Numbers of men tried to put it out, but in vain. It was some time before those at the far end of the room realised what was happening. The band kept playing so as to avoid alarm, but on seeing the emperor rush in and carry out his wife, a panic seized on all, and the dreadful scene can hardly be imagined. Each man strove to save those he loved. The windows being open gave many exits, but, alas! there were many casualties. The emperor was about everywhere, directing measures for putting out the fire and helping to carry people out. The fire engines were tardy in arriving, and when all the draperies were alight, the flames spread with such rapidity that soon the ballroom was completely burned, and the roof fell in. The cries of distress were fearful; women calling for their daughters, husbands seeking for their wives, from every part of the garden.

The beautiful sister-in-law of the Austrian Ambassador was seen rushing out of the ballroom to search for her daughters, who were, she knew, in the garden, when as she went out of the door, a candelabra fell on her head and she was killed instantly. The Queen of Naples had fainted in the middle of the crowd and was found by the King of

Würtemberg, who lifted and carried her out. Many ladies with their clothes on fire ran about the garden demented, and died in fearful agony. One poor lady was found sitting astride on a wall of the garden and never could explain how she got there.

In the meantime the flames were rapidly sweeping towards the embassy itself, where many had taken refuge, and the emperor's whole attention was directed to preventing the fire gaining ground. Numbers of troops arrived in succession to help, also General Hulin, the Governor of Paris, the Prefect of the Seine, and the head of the fire brigade, who began to apologise for his men not being in readiness to come earlier. "I know!—I know!" the emperor said sharply, "but this is not the moment for fault-finding. I will see to it all tomorrow."

Under Napoleon's orders they formed a chain in which all—kings, princes, dukes, French and foreigners—joined hands, taking off their coats and turning up their sleeves. The chain stretched right away to the other side of the street, and in this way space was left clear for the fire engines and the soldiers, who kept cutting away all communications with the embassy. Notwithstanding all efforts, the flames gained ground and the building would have been doomed had not Providence intervened. A fearful storm suddenly burst like an auxiliary force on the vast furnace, with such torrents of rain that lasted long enough to stifle the flames. Napoleon did not retire till the early morning, when it was certain all was safe. The crowds then dispersed, and only the soldiers and functionaries, whose duty it was to search in the ashes for lost articles, remained on the sad spot.

It is impossible to enumerate the quantity of precious articles which were found. Decorations of every order in Europe, watches, gold and jewelled snuff-boxes, and precious jewellery of all kinds. Everything, by the emperor's orders, was placed under the care of the Duc de Rovigo, Minister of the Police. He had given strict instructions that no stranger should pass the line of his men, who remained round the scene of the fire. One robbery was committed, owing to the Prince Kourakin, the Russian Ambassador, having fainted. He was carried into a back court of the embassy by four men, who in a shameful way, before he came to, robbed him of his jewelled buttons, his epaulettes, and his orders in diamonds—it is said, in all, to the value of 800,000 *francs*. The miscreants left him to be found by the servants, and, owing to the enormous crowd, they could not be traced.

When the storm had entirely abated and there was no longer any fear of the fire breaking out again, the Imperial Guard, who had worked so vigorously and bravely in battling with the flames, having seen that all the wounded persons had been transported to their houses, at last took some repose, and were regaled with such comestibles as had escaped the fire, while they talked over the deplorable events of the fatal night.

There was no doubt that the fire engines were late in arriving, and also were not in good order, and the chief of the police staff had not kept the crowd in order enough to satisfy the emperor. Therefore, the next morning, both he and the colonel of the fire brigade were summoned to St. Cloud, and in a very few words the emperor informed them their services would no longer be required.

The details of the terrible fire which kept pouring in gave poignant grief to Napoleon and Marie Louise. More than thirty persons were burnt alive and hundreds were seriously injured. Several ladies had thrown themselves into the ponds in the garden in their burning dresses to try to quench the flames. The poor Princess Schwartzenberg's body was so burned that she was only recognised by her brother-in-law by a little chain with a small heart of precious stones hanging from it, which he knew she always wore.

Paris was plunged into mourning and grief, and people, recalling the sad circumstance which had occurred during the festivities on the marriage of the *dauphin* to Marie Antoinette of Austria, were filled with fears of bad omen. The emperor's thoughts, doubtless, also often dwelt on this. He constantly referred to it as a warning from Providence, and that sooner or later there would be disaster in his life. He was not wrong, for it only needed three years to pass for France to fall from the seat of power and glory to which she had risen, and for the same Prince Schwartzenberg, whom Napoleon had honoured by attending his ball, to become his most violent enemy. He commanded one of the *corps d'armée* of the Allies, when the greater number of kings and princes formerly under Napoleon's sway had turned their armies against him, and though several victories were again gained by him, the fickle goddess of fortune was forsaking him, and his sun was setting.

Chasseurs à cheval (les Guides), petite et grande tenue
GARDE IMPÉRIALE.

Fusilier-Grenadier et Tirailleur-Grenadier (premier régiment)
GARDE IMPÉRIALE.

Napoleon 1815

CHAPTER 16

Waterloo

Since 1815, June 18th was and will ever be, we like to think, a day of saddest memories for France, but this year, under the circumstances of the Restoration, which makes such a painful contrast to the feelings of the people, a few details will bring more readily before them the recollection of the recent sad anniversary.

Waterloo—incomprehensible a network of unheard-of fatalities. Grouchy, Ney, d'Erlon—was there treason or only ill-fortune? Oh, poor France; astounding campaign, when in three days I foresaw three times an assured triumph slipping through my hands, notwithstanding that I had mapped out everything for the best. I had annihilated my enemies at Ligny; I saw them crushed at Waterloo if only every one had done their duty—if my orders had even been carried out accurately. Singular defeat, when notwithstanding the most horrible catastrophe, the glory of the vanquished did not suffer, nor was that of the victor augmented. The memory of the first will survive its destruction; the memory of the second will perhaps be lost in its triumph. It will be spoken of for centuries. Posterity will do me justice!

These were the words which Napoleon spoke on his dying bed at St. Helena.

On June 12th, 1815, accompanied by his grand marshal, the emperor left Paris to proceed to his headquarters at Beaumont, where all his staff were already assembled. In getting into his carriage, he smiled on his attendants, who were waiting in the hall of the Tuileries to bid him farewell.

Sirs, you cannot have been to bed! *Adieu, adieu.* The pear is ripe.

This time it is a death-duel between me and Europe. I hope soon to see you all again—*adieu!*

On the 13th, the emperor was at Avesnes, and on the 14th he arrived at Beaumont. Here his army was camped in three divisions; it consisted of 122,000 men, with 350 pieces of cannon.

On the evening of that day he issued the following proclamation, which he dictated himself, and, like Caesar and Augustus, Napoleon never missed an opportunity to recall past events, and in this way to consecrate present ones.

Today is the anniversary of Marengo and of Friedland, which twice decided the fate of Europe. Then, as after Austerlitz, and after Wagram, we were too generous. At Jena, against these same Prussians, now so arrogant, you were one against two; at Montmirail one against three—the idiots. One moment of prosperity has blinded them, but to humiliate the people of France is not in their power. If they enter. France, they will find their graves. To any Frenchman who has a heart, the moment has come to conquer or to die.

These noble sentiments fired the souls of his men, and never did their zeal to fight foreshadow a more sure victory.

On June 15th, at daybreak, the three columns of the French Army moved forward and the fight began. At several points the Prussians were completely repulsed. Charleroi was taken, and during the night of the 15th the whole of the French Army crossed the Sambre and bivouacked in a square of forty *lieues*, with the enemy's armies, who were stupefied by the cleverness and agility of Napoleon's movements, surrounding them. This first success was all the more remarkable, as during that night General Bourmont deserted from the army. At this news the emperor made changes in the plan of the attack for the next day which his desertion rendered necessary. It is said that the emperor had an instinct that Bourmont would fail him, and had refused him the command of a division which he had begged to have. Bourmont was in despair at not serving, and it was only through Marshal Ney, who gave the emperor a guarantee of his faithfulness, that he gave him a command.

On the night of June 14th Ney received orders from the emperor to occupy at daybreak, with the 40,000 men which he commanded, the position of Quatre Bras, on the way to Brussels, guarding at the same time those of Nivelle and Namur; but just as the prince was forming his army to execute this order, a cannonade, which he heard on his right flank, made him hesitate, showing that the Allies had reappeared at these points, and he halted to wait for further instructions from the emperor. The emperor, however, gently blaming him for having lost such precious time in carrying out his orders, commanded him to advance at once.

At 2 o'clock in the afternoon the emperor ordered a change of front on Fleurus, and everything foretold a speedy battle with the Prussians. Count Gerard approached him to ask for instructions with regard to the attack on the village of Ligny, and Napoleon replied: "Most likely in three hours from now the fate of the battle will be decided; it depends on Ney. If he executes my orders, the Prussian army will have a great defeat—they will be caught in a trap."

It is well known that in this battle General Gerard won new glory, and at the end of the day, Napoleon said: "I shall raise Gerard to the rank of Marshal."

Towards 4 o'clock, when both the armies were pressing against each other on all sides, and while hundreds of cannons made the earth tremble, the emperor exclaimed: "If this continues one hour longer, there will only be the French Army left standing in the plain."

A few minutes afterwards he gave General Dorsenne, commanding a division of grenadiers of the *"vieille garde,"* the order to charge with one of his battalions a *"briqueterie,"* behind which were massed a good number of Prussians. The movement was executed in a moment, and the Prussians were destroyed by the stream of fire which was poured on them, and the position was taken.

On seeing the Guards' brilliant action carried out so bravely and calmly, Napoleon turned to a general, and said: "These are brave men who can well be an example to all my young soldiers, and the grumblers will never forgive them for having done what they have without them."

Towards the end of the action, Field-Marshal Blücher, in a charge of the *cuirassiers* of the Division Delort, was thrown from his horse, but our cavalry continued their attack without noticing the accident. In great pain, he was able at last, though with difficulty, to get on a horse of a Hanoverian dragoon, and made his escape.

In the evening, the emperor went through the lines of some of the regiments who had been fighting the whole day. A few words, a smile, a shake of the hand, a salute, a nod, were sufficient to recompense the brave men who had won the victory. The number of killed and wounded on the enemy's side was considerable, and all their war material, seventy cannons and ten flags, remained in our hands.

The following day, the 17th, Marshal Ney, having had the order to attack the rear of the English Army, commanded Count Lobau to press on by the main road towards the farm of Quatre Bras. Napoleon, seeing that the farm was still occupied by the enemy, and that not a moment must be lost, sent mounted messengers to Ney to hasten on with all his strength to dislodge the enemy from this strong position.

The battle then raged with violent fury. Ney's troops were slow in coming up; the emperor kept sending messengers to hasten them on. The battle continued. Napoleon took up his position on his charger at the top of a small hill, whence he could see everything. He had only been there a few minutes, when two or three cannon-balls fell at his feet and covered him with dust; he then changed his position, saying: "I see the time has come to finish all this." He had hardly spoken when another ball fell within three feet of him, and killed an officer close by, his body rolling under the feet of Napoleon's horse. A moment afterwards, Count d'Erlon arrived on the spot, and soon after him Generals Reil and Ney. "At last," said the emperor, at once reproaching the latter for being so slow in his movements, saying angrily: "You have made us lose three precious hours."

Ney, who indeed had not been less brave or less devoted to Napoleon that day than during the whole of his glorious and fine career, seemed as if struck by some strange hallucination, replied: "Sire, I thought that the Duke of Wellington ..."

"*Monsieur* the marshal, you should not have believed anything but what I told you." Then he added in a quiet voice: "And what about your *protégé*, Bourmont, whom you so cared for?"

"Sire, he appeared to be so devoted; I would have answered for him as for myself."

"There, there, *monsieur* the marshal, those who are blue remain blue; those who are white remain white," and the emperor galloped swiftly off to another place.

The result of all the delays ended in the advance guard of the French Army not arriving at Waterloo on the 17th until 6 o'clock in the evening. Napoleon, therefore, had not time to make the great attack he had contemplated. It was then that he exclaimed, pointing to the sun: "What would I not give today to have the power of Joshua to retard the sunset for at least two hours."

The heat on the 18th was excessive, but the weather was dull.

The soldiers, overcome with fatigue, and soaked by the torrential rain which fell all through the night, saluted the day, which, alas, for most of them was to be the last of their life, with their ordinary *"vivats."* Words of command in the distance and the noise of the thunder of the cannons were all the sounds that were heard on the plain. The French Army was only composed of 69,000 men on account of the absence of the *"corps d'armée"* under Grouchy. In the army of Wellington alone there were 100,000 men. The emperor considered his troops superior in strength though inferior in number. Wellington had only half English soldiers under him, while in our ranks French, and French alone, were making common cause for glory under the same flag. Therefore, Napoleon was full of confidence and in a very good humour.

Thus, while giving numerous orders, he spoke gaily to the officers of his staff who were near him. He interrogated any prisoners of high rank who passed. Being excessively thirsty, he asked for something to drink. The supplies were too far off to procure anything, and with difficulty a bottle of *"vin du pays"* was brought him by Bertrand, who handed him a glass of it, saying: "I fear your Majesty will find this wine rather sour; it is last year's."

"Last year's!" the emperor repeated gaily; "say rather of next year." All this time, at each moment, officers kept arriving with reports of the enemy and of the course of the battle.

Napoleon decided to turn the left wing of the enemy so as to form a junction with the army corps of Grouchy, whose arrival he awaited with extreme impatience. He knew that this general had bivouacked at Gembloux, and that according to the order transmitted to him at four in the morning he should have attacked Wavres and entirely destroyed the remainder of Blücher's army; but Napoleon did not know of the junction of Bulow with the prince, a junction which had been effected during the night, without having been prevented by Grouchy. Napoleon only heard of it suddenly through a Hanoverian prisoner. The news of the uniting of these two generals greatly disturbed him, and, turning to the Duke of Dalmatia, who was close to him, said:

"This morning we had ninety chances in our favour; Bulow's junction with Blücher makes us lose thirty, but we have still sixty to forty; if Grouchy repairs the mistakes which he has made, our victory will yet be decisive."

It was now 11 o'clock. Napoleon gave Marshal Ney the order to open a heavy fire and to seize the position of Haye-Sainte. At once a heavy cannonade was heard from 150 cannons on our side. The

WELLINGTON: A SKETCH
TAKEN AT THE CEREMONY OF INAUGURATION AT OXFORD, 1852

house of Haye-Sainte, situated in a corner of the valley, was taken and retaken many times, under the eye of the Emperor, with great fury on both sides. At last, at 3 o'clock, it remained in our possession; our enemies had spent all their ammunition and most of them were killed. The battle raged at all the other points. Towards 5 o'clock the English army made a movement towards the road to Brussels, as if to be ready there in case of our retreat. The right of Wellington's army and the left of Blücher's were at once assaulted with success by our troops, and cries of victory already resounded from our brave men. "All this is too premature," Napoleon said coldly. "We do not yet see anything of Grouchy. In the meantime, we must retain what we have gained." And the battle continued.

At 7 o'clock the French Army was at last master of the field of battle, after unheard-of deeds of valour. At this moment a slight cannonade made itself heard in the direction of Waterloo. "That is Grouchy," exclaimed the emperor. In a moment all the field-glasses of the staff were directed towards that point, but the atmosphere was so thick that nothing could be distinguished. Napoleon dispatched an officer in the direction of Wavre, but he soon returned in hot haste, and, rushing to the emperor, said in an excited tone: "Sire, it is the Prussians who are approaching."

"That is impossible," replied the emperor, in an indifferent tone.

"Sire, I have seen them as clearly as I have the honour to see your Majesty," and the officer turned and took his place among the staff.

Half an hour afterwards the first column of Prussian troops detached themselves and rapidly advanced towards our left wing, guided by a peasant from the environs of Frischemont, who had told their chief that if they followed his directions, they would destroy us all. It was at this moment that Napoleon recognised the certainty that Blücher was attacking him with 150,000 Prussians. He turned very pale, and said: "His news was correct."

Then the third and last battle began. The emperor well knew the extent of the danger which surrounded him. The sun had set on the horizon. The Guards were not yet in the fray; they could fight for the last time and die. Napoleon took command. A terrible cannonade again broke forth. Blücher advanced. A division charged against the Prussian column; this division was overcome under the eyes of the emperor, whose surprise and impatience were extreme. "These Prussians," he exclaimed, hitting his boot with his whip—"oh, these Prussians, they should have been beaten an hour ago!"

He immediately ordered four squadrons of the Guards to charge. Two thousand of the *élite* of them and of dragoons threw themselves with bent heads on the solid mass of the enemy. The fearful noise was like that of numberless blacksmiths at work. It was the blows of the swords falling on the helmets and on the *cuirasses*. But what could these four squadrons do against 12,000 fresh troops? It was at this moment that, it is said, the fatal cry was heard of "*Sauve qui peut.*" But to counteract it, these sublime words, "The Guards die but never surrender," were spoken either by Cambronne, already seriously wounded, or by Dorsenne or Michel, both killed at the same time. Perhaps whoever pronounced them would not have allowed himself to survive them. However, on a hill called Mont St. Jean, where Napoleon had retired, a last reserve still remained unshaken in the midst of the tumult all round.

The emperor had taken up his place in the midst of his brave soldiers; he had a sword in his hand, and was one of them. His old companions, incapable of trembling for their own lives, were alarmed at the dangers of their emperor, and implored him to return to a place of safety. "Sire," they said, "return; this is no place for you." Napoleon paid no attention, and, after forming a squadron with his grenadiers, he himself gave the order to fire. But the officers surrounding him, seized the bridle of his horse, and drew him back; then pressing round their "eagle" and, bidding Napoleon a last farewell, they cried: "*Vive l'Empereur!*" and precipitated themselves into the thick of the battle. In this regiment were many victors of Austerlitz, Jena, and Wagram. Prussians, Russians, Saxons, English, Austrians—all suspended their cry of victory to repulse the further attack; alas, the last one by the French!

When one thinks that only 8,000 men, weakened by fatigue, fought during five hours on unequal and stony ground against an army of 130,000, it cannot be wondered at, that, notwithstanding all their bravery, they were nearly all killed; only 1,000 men were left out of the 8,000. Many indeed preferred to die by their own hands rather than by that of the Prussians. The latter lost 20,000 before the battle ended, which proves the desperate courage with which the vanquished fought. Surely it is to them the palm of honour is due. The retreat of the remainder of the army was carried out by fresh prodigies of endurance. The roads were torn up, and a general *pêle-mêle* arose among the cavalry, infantry, and artillery. General Duhesme, one of the bravest of the army, was taken prisoner by the Prussians, who killed him. For a long time Napoleon refused to move, saying he wished also to die; and at last Bertrand, ever near him, implored him to leave; but Napoleon once more seized his arm convulsively, and said: "No, no, Bertrand, my place is here!"

It was not until eleven at night that the emperor agreed to Bertrand's wish, his ever faithful companion, who never left him till he had closed his eyes for ever, 3,000 *lieues* from France.

At his last moment, when he pronounced the words which we cited at the beginning of this article, he was far from foreseeing that an epoch would arise when the anniversary of this great national disaster would be celebrated by joyous festivities in Paris and in London.

Tambour-Major et Tambour des Grenadiers à pied
GARDE IMPÉRIALE.

Grenadier à cheval, soldat, grande tenue, et Officier, petite tenue.
GARDE IMPÉRIALE.

Chapter 17

The Emperor's Mother

"The most interesting day of my life," the Countess d'Orsay said to me one day, when we were talking over Madame Laetitia, the emperor's mother, "and which touched me more than anything, was that on which I paid her a visit in Rome, not having seen her since she was in the zenith of her son's fame. She then lived in a house near Paris, where she led a quiet and simple life, as pomp and grandeur had no attraction for her. After Napoleon's defeat and death she went to live in Rome, and it was there I found her in the spring after that sad event, when I was spending a few weeks in the Eternal City. It was on one of those lovely mornings when Italy's sun and the perfumes of its myriad flowers and shrubs bring joy into one's heart, and the contrast was all the greater when I entered the Palace Rinuccini, a fine but gloomy building in the Place de Venise.

"The door closed behind me with a dull metallic sound which re-echoed a hundred times through the lofty hall. It was as cool as the interior of a cave notwithstanding the intense heat outside. Following the servant through many rooms, he at last ushered me into a small one, where Madame Laetitia's lady companion was sitting. On hearing my name, she rose and welcomed me, and hastened to go and see if her mistress was well enough to see me, for she was, alas, very feeble, and had never recovered from a fall she had in the gardens of the Villa Borghese two years before. Her companion soon returned and bade me follow her into a *salon*, where Madame Laetitia was lying on a small bedstead. She raised herself on her cushions when I approached her, and fixed her large, vacant eyes on mine.

"I can assure you I did not pity her, knowing that all she would have seen on the walls of that room would have deeply saddened her, as they were covered with pictures of battles, in many of which

Napoleon and his brave soldiers figured, and how they would have reopened the wounds of an agonised and banished mother. Tears came into my eyes, and it needed great self-control not to let the unhappy lady guess from my voice all that I was feeling for her, in being surrounded by such mementoes of victories and defeats. She held out her hands and drew me towards her. After a few questions with regard to my journey all the talk turned on Paris. Her voice was very feeble, and it grieved me to the heart to see this poor neglected woman lying on the bed from which she would never rise again, and not one member of her numerous family with her.

"It is very, very sad," she said, "to live as I live, bedridden and in pain, far from my children and no distractions for my sad thoughts. Till my accident occurred, I was able sometimes to attend Mass at the nearest church, and to walk in the gardens of the Villa Borghese. It was the French who made the beautiful drive on the Monte Pincio, and I seem to be breathing the air of France on that lovely hill. Attending the French church of La Trinità di Monte gave me great peace and happiness, with its simple and beautiful services. I envy those who climb the steps from the Piazza di Spagna on a beautiful day like this. I feel my room is full of sunshine; I fancy I can see its reflection through the windows; the sun is my only friend."

With all respect and attention I tried to turn her mind from her desolate thoughts, and to talk of the glory which surrounded her name, and I said to her: "You must be proud at having been selected among all the women of Europe to give to the world its grandest gift."

This remark caused a smile to spread over her faded features. "Yes," she said—"yes, it is indeed the thought of my son which consoles me. I see him perpetually before me, but not as emperor. The great man that I see is my son, Bonaparte, as a child, when he only belonged to me, his mother. That is how I know him. What a happy time! One evening, when he was between eight and nine years of age, I saw him walking in the garden with the air of a man who was meditating on some abstruse subject. It was raining hard. His brothers were playing in the house. I knocked at the window and called him several times and beckoned him to come in. He shrugged his little shoulders (a sign of ill-humour with him) and continued walking. The rain had stuck his hair on to his forehead.

"He did not seem to mind the storm, and continued walking with bare head. One clap of thunder broke, which made him shake, more from nervousness than fear. Then he crossed his little arms and looked steadfastly at the sky to await with courage the next clap of thunder. I sent a servant out to call him in, but he bade her tell me that he was so hot he was trying to get cool. It was not till the end of the storm that he came into the house.

"'You behave very badly in disobeying me.'

"'I disobeyed unwillingly,' he replied; 'I do not know what made me remain in the garden, but as I mean to be a soldier, I must accustom myself to rain and bad weather. I am not a little girl; I am a man.'

"'You are only a child, my boy, and a very disobedient one. If you wish to be a soldier, you will have to obey orders.'

"'But it is I who will give orders,' he said, with a proud look; 'others will have to obey me.'

"'Before commanding, you will have to be obedient for a long time—generals are not made in a moment.'

"He came up to me and took my hand in his small one and gave me a kiss, as if to say I was right, but he would not admit it, so proud he was at that age.

"'What were you thinking about when you were walking about in the rain?'

"'I do not know; I cannot recollect; I thought of so many things. Oh, yes, I was trying to remember a dream I had last night—a dream that pleased me. I dreamt that I was a bishop. It is very grand, *ma mère*, is it not, to be a bishop? Do they go to the wars?'

"'No, my son, that is forbidden them.'

"'Then I will be a simple soldier when I am no longer a child. At fifteen one is no longer a child, is one?'

"'Yes, still, for a little longer.'

"He thought deeply, and then looked up at the ceiling, and said: 'At fifteen I shall be a man,' and he slipped away from me and ran upstairs."

The angel mother who related me all this stopped, and her pale lips trembled. I well understood all that was passing through her mind when episodes of her beloved son's life passed through it. I thanked her with deep feeling, and kissed her hand and bade her farewell, leaving, with deepest feelings of respect and sympathy, the forlorn mother who was ending her days in a strange land, with only the recollection of those she loved to console her.

ALSO FROM LEONAUR
AVAILABLE IN SOFTCOVER OR HARDCOVER WITH DUST JACKET

THE FALL OF THE MOGHUL EMPIRE OF HINDUSTAN *by H. G. Keene*—By the beginning of the nineteenth century, as British and Indian armies under Lake and Wellesley dominated the scene, a little over half a century of conflict brought the Moghul Empire to its knees.

LADY SALE'S AFGHANISTAN *by Florentia Sale*—An Indomitable Victorian Lady's Account of the Retreat from Kabul During the First Afghan War.

THE CAMPAIGN OF MAGENTA AND SOLFERINO 1859 *by Harold Carmichael Wylly*—The Decisive Conflict for the Unification of Italy.

FRENCH'S CAVALRY CAMPAIGN *by J. G. Maydon*—A Special Correspondent's View of British Army Mounted Troops During the Boer War.

CAVALRY AT WATERLOO *by Sir Evelyn Wood*—British Mounted Troops During the Campaign of 1815.

THE SUBALTERN *by George Robert Gleig*—The Experiences of an Officer of the 85th Light Infantry During the Peninsular War.

NAPOLEON AT BAY, 1814 *by F. Loraine Petre*—The Campaigns to the Fall of the First Empire.

NAPOLEON AND THE CAMPAIGN OF 1806 *by Colonel Vachée*—The Napoleonic Method of Organisation and Command to the Battles of Jena & Auerstädt.

THE COMPLETE ADVENTURES IN THE CONNAUGHT RANGERS *by William Grattan*—The 88th Regiment during the Napoleonic Wars by a Serving Officer.

BUGLER AND OFFICER OF THE RIFLES *by William Green & Harry Smith*—With the 95th (Rifles) during the Peninsular & Waterloo Campaigns of the Napoleonic Wars.

NAPOLEONIC WAR STORIES *by Sir Arthur Quiller-Couch*—Tales of soldiers, spies, battles & sieges from the Peninsular & Waterloo campaingns.

CAPTAIN OF THE 95TH (RIFLES) *by Jonathan Leach*—An officer of Wellington's sharpshooters during the Peninsular, South of France and Waterloo campaigns of the Napoleonic wars.

RIFLEMAN COSTELLO *by Edward Costello*—The adventures of a soldier of the 95th (Rifles) in the Peninsular & Waterloo Campaigns of the Napoleonic wars.

AVAILABLE ONLINE AT **www.leonaur.com**
AND FROM ALL GOOD BOOK STORES

ALSO FROM LEONAUR
AVAILABLE IN SOFTCOVER OR HARDCOVER WITH DUST JACKET

AT THEM WITH THE BAYONET by *Donald F. Featherstone*—The first Anglo-Sikh War 1845-1846.

STEPHEN CRANE'S BATTLES by *Stephen Crane*—Nine Decisive Battles Recounted by the Author of 'The Red Badge of Courage'.

THE GURKHA WAR by *H. T. Prinsep*—The Anglo-Nepalese Conflict in North East India 1814-1816.

FIRE & BLOOD by *G. R. Gleig*—The burning of Washington & the battle of New Orleans, 1814, through the eyes of a young British soldier.

SOUND ADVANCE! by *Joseph Anderson*—Experiences of an officer of HM 50th regiment in Australia, Burma & the Gwalior war.

THE CAMPAIGN OF THE INDUS by *Thomas Holdsworth*—Experiences of a British Officer of the 2nd (Queen's Royal) Regiment in the Campaign to Place Shah Shuja on the Throne of Afghanistan 1838 - 1840.

WITH THE MADRAS EUROPEAN REGIMENT IN BURMA by *John Butler*—The Experiences of an Officer of the Honourable East India Company's Army During the First Anglo-Burmese War 1824 - 1826.

IN ZULULAND WITH THE BRITISH ARMY by *Charles L. Norris-Newman*—The Anglo-Zulu war of 1879 through the first-hand experiences of a special correspondent.

BESIEGED IN LUCKNOW by *Martin Richard Gubbins*—The first Anglo-Sikh War 1845-1846.

A TIGER ON HORSEBACK by *L. March Phillips*—The Experiences of a Trooper & Officer of Rimington's Guides - The Tigers - during the Anglo-Boer war 1899 - 1902.

SEPOYS, SIEGE & STORM by *Charles John Griffiths*—The Experiences of a young officer of H.M.'s 61st Regiment at Ferozepore, Delhi ridge and at the fall of Delhi during the Indian mutiny 1857.

CAMPAIGNING IN ZULULAND by *W. E. Montague*—Experiences on campaign during the Zulu war of 1879 with the 94th Regiment.

THE STORY OF THE GUIDES by *G.J. Younghusband*—The Exploits of the Soldiers of the famous Indian Army Regiment from the northwest frontier 1847 - 1900.

AVAILABLE ONLINE AT **www.leonaur.com**
AND FROM ALL GOOD BOOK STORES

ALSO FROM LEONAUR
AVAILABLE IN SOFTCOVER OR HARDCOVER WITH DUST JACKET

ZULU:1879 *by D.C.F. Moodie & the Leonaur Editors*—The Anglo-Zulu War of 1879 from contemporary sources: First Hand Accounts, Interviews, Dispatches, Official Documents & Newspaper Reports.

THE RED DRAGOON *by W.J. Adams*—With the 7th Dragoon Guards in the Cape of Good Hope against the Boers & the Kaffir tribes during the 'war of the axe' 1843-48'.

THE RECOLLECTIONS OF SKINNER OF SKINNER'S HORSE *by James Skinner*—James Skinner and his 'Yellow Boys' Irregular cavalry in the wars of India between the British, Mahratta, Rajput, Mogul, Sikh & Pindarree Forces.

A CAVALRY OFFICER DURING THE SEPOY REVOLT *by A. R. D. Mackenzie*—Experiences with the 3rd Bengal Light Cavalry, the Guides and Sikh Irregular Cavalry from the outbreak to Delhi and Lucknow.

A NORFOLK SOLDIER IN THE FIRST SIKH WAR *by J W Baldwin*—Experiences of a private of H.M. 9th Regiment of Foot in the battles for the Punjab, India 1845-6.

TOMMY ATKINS' WAR STORIES: 14 FIRST HAND ACCOUNTS—Fourteen first hand accounts from the ranks of the British Army during Queen Victoria's Empire.

THE WATERLOO LETTERS *by H. T. Siborne*—Accounts of the Battle by British Officers for its Foremost Historian.

NEY: GENERAL OF CAVALRY VOLUME 1—1769-1799 *by Antoine Bulos*—The Early Career of a Marshal of the First Empire.

NEY: MARSHAL OF FRANCE VOLUME 2—1799-1805 *by Antoine Bulos*—The Early Career of a Marshal of the First Empire.

AIDE-DE-CAMP TO NAPOLEON *by Philippe-Paul de Ségur*—For anyone interested in the Napoleonic Wars this book, written by one who was intimate with the strategies and machinations of the Emperor, will be essential reading.

TWILIGHT OF EMPIRE *by Sir Thomas Ussher & Sir George Cockburn*—Two accounts of Napoleon's Journeys in Exile to Elba and St. Helena: Narrative of Events by Sir Thomas Ussher & Napoleon's Last Voyage: Extract of a diary by Sir George Cockburn.

PRIVATE WHEELER *by William Wheeler*—The letters of a soldier of the 51st Light Infantry during the Peninsular War & at Waterloo.

AVAILABLE ONLINE AT **www.leonaur.com**
AND FROM ALL GOOD BOOK STORES

www.ingramcontent.com/pod-product-compliance
Lightning Source LLC
Chambersburg PA
CBHW021004090426
42738CB00007B/654